Index

COACHING FOR A LIFE WELL-LIVED

"Life is a continuous learning,
Keep learning continuous"

SUDHIR DASAMANTHARAO

ISBN 979-8-89610-670-8

PART 1

FOUNDATIONS OF A FULFILLED LIFE

Chapter 1

What is Life All About?

"Life is what happens when you're busy making other plans," John Lennon once said. He,might have been onto something, but I'd argue life is also what happens when you're willing to abandon those plans altogether. Sometimes, the most real moments of growth happen when we let go of where we thought we were headed and allow ourselves to follow a different path—one that we never saw coming.

Life as a Journey

When I was growing up in a large joint family, life seemed like it was all about achievements - a series of milestones. Do well in school. Graduate from college. Get a respectable job. Get married. Buy a house. Make the family proud. It felt like there was always another goal to reach, another box to tick off. But something about that never quite sat right with me, even as a child. Even as a kid, when my uncles and aunts would lean down and ask me the typical question with a smile, "What do you want to be when you grow up?" I found myself hesitating, my mind racing between becoming an astronaut exploring the vastness of space, a rockstar electrifying crowds with powerful music, or perhaps something even more fantastical and beyond ordinary expectations. The thought of having my life planned out, with every milestone lined up in order, felt too restricting. How could anyone want me to stick to a path set before I even got to figure out who I am and what I really want from life?

In our family, we were taught the importance of sharing and caring, of building strong bonds that would last a lifetime. Looking back, those early lessons weren't about reaching milestones but about the experiences we created together—the stories we shared, the values that were passed down. It wasn't the achievements that stayed with me; it was the everyday interactions, the laughter, the learning that took place around the dinner table.

As I moved through life, those early experiences began to shape my perspective. I started to see that life isn't a checklist of goals. It's not just about getting from one point to the next. It's about how we grow and change along the way. Each phase of life, every twist and turn, brings with it the chance to evolve, to learn something new, and to become a little more of who we're meant to be.

This realization hit home for me when I transitioned from finance to roles in quality and project management. At first, I thought of these shifts as just another step in my career—a way to climb higher, earn more, and achieve success. But over time, I began to see these changes differently. They weren't just about acquiring new skills or moving up the ladder. They were about evolving as a person. Every challenge I faced, every new skill I learned, wasn't just a means to an end. It was part of a larger journey of personal growth.

Lifelong learning became a cornerstone of this journey. It wasn't just about formal education or getting more degrees. It was about staying curious, being open to new ideas, and, perhaps most importantly, being willing to let go of old ways of thinking that no longer served me. This mindset helped me through the ups and downs of life—those moments when everything seemed to change at once, forcing me to rethink and adapt.

But the journey wasn't always straightforward. There were times when I felt stuck, unsure of which direction to take. That's when I discovered the value of life coaching. Unlike traditional advice, which often tells you what to do, coaching helped me uncover my own answers. It wasn't about someone else giving me a plan to follow. It was about being guided to ask the right questions, to explore my own thoughts and feelings, and to find my own path forward.

Life coaching didn't provide a clear-cut route, but it offered me the clarity I needed to move forward with confidence. It helped me understand that the real value of life isn't in reaching a final destination but in the process of growing, learning, and evolving with each experience.

Life's Core Pillars

As I thought more about my journey, I realized life coaching was more than just advice on career moves or personal issues. It showed me what really matters in life. Peeling back the layers, I discovered a few basic principles that had always been there, even if I hadn't always seen them. The best things in life, right? These principles - relationships, learning, experiences, and emotions - are what make life meaningful and fulfilling.

Relationships: The Heartbeat of Life

From the moment we are born, relationships become an intrinsic part of who we are. In my life, this was more evident than ever, growing up in a large joint family. My father had five brothers and five sisters, and I grew up alongside my sisters and 25 cousins. The house was always full—full of laughter, full of conversations, full of life. From a young age, I learned the importance of sharing and caring, not just as values, but as daily practices. We didn't have much, but whatever we had, we shared. If one of us was in trouble, we all stood together. If an outsider tried to harm a family member, we'd rally around them without hesitation.

These early experiences taught me something fundamental: relationships are the bedrock of a fulfilling life. The bonds we create with others—whether they're with family, friends, or colleagues—give our lives meaning. They provide us with a sense of belonging and support, especially in times of need. And they bring joy, as we celebrate life's milestones together.

As I grew older and entered the professional world, I saw this same principle at work in a different context. Building a successful career wasn't just about networking or knowing the right people. It was about forming real, meaningful connections—relationships based on trust, mutual respect, and a genuine interest in each other's well-being. These were the relationships that opened doors, provided support during tough times, and led to true collaboration and success.

But maintaining these relationships takes effort, especially in today's fast-paced world. We often get caught up in the demands of daily life, telling ourselves that we'll reach out to that old friend or visit a family member when things slow down. But life doesn't slow down, and before we know it, years have passed. This is why it's so important to prioritize the relationships that matter. It's not about finding the time; it's about making the time.

One of the most valuable lessons I've learned is that relationships aren't just about being there during the good times. They're about showing up during the tough times, too. True relationships are those that can weather the storms— where both people are willing to put in the effort, even when it's hard. These are the relationships that add real value to our lives, that provide us with the emotional resilience to keep going when things get tough.

In coaching, this understanding of relationships becomes crucial. A life coach helps you recognize the importance of these connections and guides you in nurturing them. Coaching is not just about personal achievements or professional milestones; it's about understanding that the quality of your relationships often determines the quality of your life.

But again, it's important to remember that not every connection will be a deep one, and that's okay. What matters is focusing on the quality of the relationships we choose to invest in. Surround yourself with people who lift you up, who are honest and genuine, and who will stand by you through life's ups and downs. These are the relationships that will enrich your life, providing you with a sense of purpose and fulfillment that goes far beyond individual achievements.

In the end, life is about the connections we make and the bonds we build. When we look back, it's not the accolades or material successes that we'll cherish most, but the relationships we've nurtured—the people who were there for us, who shared in our joys and sorrows, and who made our journey through life a little bit brighter.

Learning: The Never-Ending Journey

When we think of learning, formal education often comes to mind—degrees, certifications, qualifications. But true learning extends far beyond the classroom. It's not just about what we're taught; it's about what life teaches us every single day. From our own experiences and the experiences of others, learning is a continuous process that we carry with us throughout our lives.

Growing up, I was always encouraged to study hard, get good grades, and earn my qualifications. But as I moved through different stages of life, I realized that learning is more than just acquiring knowledge. It's about understanding how to use that knowledge in meaningful ways. It's about staying curious, open-minded, and being willing to let go of ideas that no longer serve us.

One of the most important lessons I've learned is that life is always teaching us something new. Whether we realize it or not, every situation we encounter has something to offer. Sometimes the lessons are gentle, like learning patience through a long wait. Other times, they're more challenging, pushing us to confront our mistakes and learn from them. But in every case, there's something valuable to take away—if we're willing to see it.

I remember a time in my career when I was completely focused on accumulating certifications, thinking that each new qualification would inch me closer to success. But soon enough, I realized that those certificates were just one piece of the puzzle. The true value came when I began applying what I had learned—when I used that knowledge to solve real-world problems and create meaningful impact in my work. It was in those moments that I truly understood what learning is all about. As I would often remind myself: **"Life is a continuous learning: keep learning continuous."** It's not just about gathering information, but about using it to make changes and growing from those experiences.

Just as important as learning is the ability to unlearn. As we go through life, our views and perspectives evolve. What once seemed true may no longer apply, and being able to adapt to new ideas is crucial. This flexibility in thinking, the ability to reassess and adjust our beliefs, is what allows us to keep moving forward.

In life coaching, this commitment to continuous learning is essential. A coach doesn't just help you achieve your goals; they encourage you to keep learning from every experience, to see each moment as an opportunity to grow. Whether you're dealing with a setback or reaching a milestone, the focus is always on what you can learn and how that learning can help you grow.

As we progress through life, it's easy to chase after success—promotions, awards, financial gain. But the people who find true fulfillment are often those who never stop learning. They understand that life isn't just about reaching goals; it's about learning from every experience, using each one as a chance to grow wiser. Learning shapes who we are. It helps us gain clarity and direction, guiding us to become the person we want to be, rather than the person others expect us to be.

Experiences and Memories

Life has a way of presenting us with firsts—our first day at school, our first job, our first time traveling alone. These first-time experiences often leave a lasting impression, creating memories that we carry with us throughout our lives. Whether these moments are filled with excitement, anxiety, or even fear, they have a unique ability to shape our understanding of the world and ourselves.

Growing up, my first day of school was more than just the start of my education. It was the beginning of a journey into a world beyond home, teaching me resilience and the ability to adapt. These are lessons that have stayed with me long after the details of that day have faded.

As we progress through life, each stage brings new experiences, adding to our collection of memories. Interestingly, we may not recall the exact amount spent on a holiday, but we remember the joy of exploring a new place, the laughter shared, and the sense of wonder. These are the moments that stay with us, reminding us of the richness of life.

In coaching, we focus on creating intentional experiences that lead to lasting memories. Life isn't just about what happens; it's about how we choose to engage with those moments. By seeking new experiences and being open to what each day offers, we can create memories that enrich our lives and the lives of others.

There's a story of a bird that carefully builds a nest, only to leave it behind when its chicks learn to fly. The nest, built with care, becomes a home for another bird—a place where new memories will be made. This story highlights the importance of creating experiences that not only shape our own lives but also positively impact others.

As we move through life, it's easy to get caught up in the future. But it's important to reflect on the memories we've created and be mindful of the experiences we're shaping today. Life is like a journey where people come and go, and what matters most is the quality of that journey and the memories we create along the way.

In the end, memories are what we carry with us. They are the moments that make life rich and meaningful.

Emotions

Emotions are what make us human. They're not just feelings we experience in reaction to events; they're the drivers of our actions, often dictating the choices we make and the paths we take. From the joy of a celebration to the sting of disappointment, emotions color every aspect of our lives. As the saying goes, "We might be the master of our own thoughts, still we are the slaves of our own emotions."

This truth reveals itself in the smallest moments. Think about a time when you've been moved to help someone simply because you felt their pain or joy. It wasn't a logical decision—it was an emotional one. Emotions connect us to others, often in ways that logic and reason can't.

Consider the story of a young boy who, out of hunger and desperation, knocked on a stranger's door and asked for a glass of water. The woman who answered saw beyond his request and, sensing his need, offered him a glass of milk instead. This simple act of kindness touched the boy deeply, far beyond the immediate quenching of his thirst. That moment stayed with him for years, shaping his belief in the goodness of people. Many years later, as a successful doctor, he found himself treating the same woman who had once helped him. When the time came to settle her medical bill, he remembered the glass of milk and wrote on the bill, "Paid in full with one glass of milk."

This story beautifully illustrates the power of emotions. A small act of kindness, driven by empathy, created a lasting bond that transcended time and circumstance. Emotions, when they come from a place of genuine care, have the power to create connections that last a lifetime.

However, emotions are not always straightforward. They can be complex, sometimes conflicting, and often difficult to manage. This is where emotional awareness becomes crucial. Understanding our emotions—recognizing them, acknowledging their impact, and learning to manage them— can significantly influence the quality of our lives. It's not just about reacting to what we feel; it's about responding in a way that aligns with our values and goals.

In coaching, this principle is essential. A life coach helps you become more aware of your emotions, not to suppress them, but to understand them and use that understanding to guide your actions. This is particularly important in moments of decision-making, where emotions can cloud judgment. Recognizing when your emotions are steering you and learning to channel them constructively can be a game-changer in both personal and professional settings.

Emotions also play a crucial role in the relationships we build. It's often the emotional connection we feel towards others that defines the strength and depth of those relationships. Whether it's a bond with a family member, a friend, or a colleague, the emotions we invest in those relationships often determine their longevity and impact on our lives.

Ultimately, life is not just about what happens to us; it's about how we feel about what happens to us. Our emotions, more than the events themselves, shape our experiences and memories. By becoming more aware of our emotions and learning to manage them effectively, we can create a life that's not only richer in experience but also more aligned with our true selves.

Afterall, while we may strive to control our thoughts, it's our emotions that often lead the way. The key is not to deny them, but to understand them, to learn from them, and to let them guide us toward the life we truly want to live.

Life revolves around the journey, not merely reaching milestones.It's shaped by our relationships, experiences, and emotions. What really forms us are the connections we make, the lessons we learn, the memories we cherish, and how we handle our feelings. True fulfillment comes from growing, adapting, and reflecting.

As you go on to explore the pages ahead, remember, life's value doesn't lie in the end points but the journey itself. It's in the everyday moments, the growth, and the meaningful relationships. Embrace learning, cherish your relationships, and listen to your emotions. By doing this, you'll lead a fulfilling life and inspire others to do the same.

Chapter 2

Coaching for Life — The Foundation of Fulfillment

Every day, we're faced with an overwhelming array of choices—career paths, lifestyle decisions, endless options at every turn. In a world that's always on and digitally driven, it's easy to confuse movement with progress. We chase milestones, accumulate achievements, yet often find ourselves questioning if we're truly moving toward what we really want. Success, without a clear sense of who we are and what we value, can feel like we're going in circles.

Eventually, the realization dawns: the most important decisions in life can't be guided solely by external advice. The answers we seek aren't found out there—they're within us, waiting to be uncovered. This is where coaching comes in. It's not about being told which path to take; it's about being guided to ask the right questions that lead you to your own path.

What is Coaching for Life?

Coaching is a term often used in discussions about personal growth, but what does it truly mean? Unlike mentoring or advising, coaching doesn't hand you ready-made answers. Instead, it empowers you to discover your own. While mentors might guide you through familiar territory, coaching encourages you to explore deeper, asking tough questions about your values, beliefs, and goals. It's not just about achieving external success; it's about making sure your actions align with what truly matters to you.

In a world saturated with quick fixes and instant solutions, coaching invites you to slow down and reflect. It's a powerful tool that helps you explore your core values, beliefs, and aspirations. Often, when we think of personal growth, we focus on the tangible—advancing in our careers, acquiring new skills, or checking off life's milestones. But true growth happens within. Coaching challenges you to ask the essential questions: What matters most to you? What drives your choices? Do your daily actions align with the person you want to become?

Coaching isn't a quick fix or a one-time solution to life's challenges. It's a vital skill for navigating life's complexities, building resilience, and maintaining perspective through ups and downs. Coaching helps you bridge the gap between where you are and where you want to be, not by giving you a set of directions, but by helping you chart your own course. It's about ensuring that every step you take is deliberate, bringing you closer to a life that genuinely reflects who you are.

Through coaching, you take responsibility for your own life. It's easy to rely on external advice, to follow someone else's path. But coaching encourages you to take ownership of your decisions, reminding you that while guidance can be helpful, the direction of your life is ultimately yours to define. This sense of ownership turns choices into commitments and transforms goals into realities.

Rather than focusing on fixed outcomes, coaching helps you view every experience as a chance to learn and grow. Setbacks aren't seen as failures but as valuable lessons that propel you forward. This shift in perspective is crucial for managing life's uncertainties, turning challenges into opportunities for personal development.

The Role of Values, Beliefs, and Goals

When you think about the decisions you make every day— whether it's choosing a career path, deciding how to spend your time, or determining what kind of relationships to build— what's guiding those choices? Often, it's our values, beliefs, and goals, whether we realize it or not. These elements act as the compass for our lives, subtly influencing every action we take. But here's the thing: if we're not conscious of them, they can lead us in directions we never intended to go.

Think of your life as a ship at sea. The waves and winds represent the daily challenges and opportunities you encounter. Your core values are the rudder, steering you through these conditions. Without a clear understanding of your values, it's easy to be tossed around, reacting to whatever comes your way. But when you know what matters most to you, you can steer with purpose, making decisions that align with who you truly are.

Identifying your core values isn't just a one-time exercise; it's an ongoing process of reflection. One effective way to start is by asking yourself a series of simple but revealing questions: What makes you feel fulfilled? What principles are you unwilling to compromise? When you look back at the decisions you've made, which ones felt most true to yourself?

Through these reflections, you begin to uncover the values that are non-negotiable for you—whether it's integrity, family, creativity, or something else entirely. Aligning your daily actions with these values isn't just about feeling good; it's about living a life that feels authentic. When your actions reflect your values, you experience a deeper sense of fulfillment and purpose.

Conversely, when there's a gap between your values and your actions, dissatisfaction often follows. It's like living someone else's life rather than your own. Coaching helps you identify where these misalignments exist and guides you to make changes that bring your life back into alignment.

While values are the rudder of your life, beliefs are the engine that drives your actions. But not all engines run smoothly—some are fueled by limiting beliefs that keep you stuck in place. These are the beliefs that tell you what you can't do, who you can't be, and where you don't belong. They're often rooted in past experiences or inherited from others through conditioning, and they have a sneaky way of holding you back without you even realizing it.

Coaching helps you bring these limiting beliefs to the surface, where they can be examined and challenged. Once you recognize a limiting belief, you can start to question its validity: Is it really true? Where did it come from? How is it serving you—or more likely, how is it not serving you?

On the other hand, empowering beliefs act like high-octane fuel, driving you toward your goals with confidence and clarity. These are the beliefs that open doors rather than close them. Through coaching, you learn to replace limiting beliefs with empowering ones, transforming your mindset and, ultimately, your life.

Once you've clarified your values and beliefs, the next step is setting goals that align with them. This is where coaching really shines. Setting goals can often feel overwhelming, especially if they're big or long-term. But when you break them down into SMART goals—Specific, Measurable, Achievable, Relevant, and Time-bound—they become much more manageable.

The beauty of the coaching process is that it doesn't just help you set these goals; it helps you turn your aspirations into actionable steps, one by one, making the journey less daunting and more achievable.

Coaching as a Life Skill

Life is full of challenges—some expected, others that catch us off guard. Coaching offers practical ways to manage these complexities. Rather than getting lost in the chaos, coaching helps you develop strategies that keep you grounded and focused. It teaches you to approach problems with clarity, allowing you to tackle them step by step instead of feeling overwhelmed by the big picture. The idea is to focus on what you can control and let go of what you can't, a skill that becomes invaluable when life gets tough.

But handling challenges is just one piece of the puzzle. True fulfillment comes from aligning your actions with what truly matters to you. It's not just about achieving goals but making sure those goals reflect who you are and what you want from life. When your daily actions align with your broader life goals, everything feels more meaningful. Coaching plays a crucial role in helping you maintain this alignment, guiding you to make choices that lead to a more fulfilling and authentic life.

What makes coaching truly powerful is its ability to transform the way you navigate life, even outside of formal sessions. The real strength of coaching lies in developing the ability to coach yourself. This means regularly reflecting on your experiences, asking yourself the right questions, and holding yourself accountable. It's about making self-assessment a habit, so you can stay on track and make adjustments as needed. Over time, this practice empowers you to handle life's ups and downs with greater ease, helping you to stay focused and resilient no matter what comes your way.

This resilience is crucial because emotional strength is what keeps you grounded when life throws curveballs. By learning to manage your emotions effectively, you prevent them from derailing you during tough times. Simple practices like journaling, mindfulness, and gratitude become powerful tools in maintaining balance and positivity. These aren't just nice-to-haves; they're essential components of a resilient mindset. By integrating these habits into your daily routine, you build a foundation of emotional strength that supports you through life's challenges, allowing you to bounce back and helping you grow stronger with each experience.

Coaching doesn't hand you clear-cut answers; rather, it steers you towards asking the right questions. It's a process of uncovering your truths, ensuring your actions reflect your values, and developing the resilience to tackle life's challenges.

Remember, it's not just reaching a final destination; it's constantly evolving into the best version of yourself. Every decision, every challenge, is an opportunity to learn, adapt, and embrace your true essence.

When you make choices with intention and purpose, you're crafting a life that's not just fulfilling, but truly your own—one step at a time.

PART 2

THE POWER
OF COACHING

Chapter 3

Beyond the Mentor: Coaching Explained

"All that we are is the result of what we have thought... If a man speaks or acts with a good thought, happiness follows him like a shadow that never leaves him."

– Buddha

Coaching starts with a simple premise: the right questions can lead you to the right answers. It's not about offering solutions or handing you a script to follow. It's about guiding you to look inward, to examine the stories you've been telling yourself, and to see if those stories are still serving you. We often live within the boundaries of what we believe we can or cannot do. But what if those beliefs are just assumptions that can be challenged and reshaped?

Think of it this way: many of the limits in life are self-imposed. The story of Buddha's transformation from a prince living in luxury to an enlightened figure isn't just a spiritual tale—it's a powerful example of questioning one's reality. He had everything that was supposed to bring happiness, but it wasn't until he faced the realities of suffering that he started asking deeper questions about life. This wasn't about seeking immediate answers but understanding the deeper truths. The same principle applies in coaching. When you start to question the narratives you've built around your capabilities and limitations, you open up possibilities you hadn't considered.

Your thoughts shape your reality. A quote often attributed to Buddha says, "All that we are is the result of what we have thought... If a man speaks or acts with a good thought, happiness follows him like a shadow that never leaves him." When you begin to see your thoughts as the architects of your actions and outcomes, you gain a new sense of power. The right kind of self-reflection helps you see where you've been stuck and where you can make meaningful changes. It's not about passive reflection; it's about engaging with these thoughts, challenging them, and actively choosing which ones will guide you forward.

Traditional advice often skips this step. It might tell you what to do without asking why. Coaching, however, encourages you to think more critically. It pushes you to challenge your assumptions and consider new perspectives. For example, if you've always believed you're not "good with numbers," what's that belief based on? An experience from childhood? A narrative you've reinforced over the years? When you challenge these assumptions, you often find they have little grounding in reality.

The psychological impact here is significant. The act of questioning and reframing your thoughts isn't just a mental exercise—it rewires your brain. You're building new neural pathways that help you approach problems more creatively and make decisions more effectively. Instead of reacting out of habit, you start responding with intention. This shift—from merely accepting what life gives you to actively shaping what you want—aligns with the idea that life doesn't hand you more than you ask for. It starts with building the mindset and habits that make you deserving of what you seek.

The Science Behind Coaching

At its core, effective coaching integrates ideas from psychology. Two key techniques often used are cognitive behavioral methods and motivational interviewing. These approaches help you shift your mindset, not by imposing new ideas but by encouraging you to see your thoughts differently.

Consider cognitive behavioral techniques. They explore how your thoughts, feelings, and actions are interconnected. If you believe that you always mess up when things get stressful, that belief can influence what you do and even make it come true. But what if you could change that belief? By breaking down this way of thinking and examining it closely, coaching can help you replace negative thoughts with constructive ones. It's not just about staying positive; it's about thinking in a smarter, more adaptive way.

Motivational interviewing, on the other hand, helps you uncover your reasons for wanting to change. It doesn't prescribe what you should do; it helps you articulate why you want to make a change. This small shift is crucial. When you understand the "why" behind your actions, you're much more likely to follow through because the change feels self-directed, not imposed.

Both techniques are grounded in the concept of neuroplasticity—the idea that our brains are continually changing based on our thoughts and experiences. When you start to think differently, you're not just shifting your mindset; you're actually rewiring your brain. The more you practice new ways of thinking, the stronger those new connections become. It's like clearing a new path in a dense forest; the more you walk it, the more defined it becomes.

Changing your mindset can indeed alter the direction of your life. It's not just a motivational phrase; it's backed by science. When you learn to think differently, you improve your ability to tackle challenges, manage stress, and interact with others. Coaching makes this shift more accessible by creating a supportive environment for personal growth. Rather than reacting to life's events, you start shaping your own experiences.

Research supports this approach. Studies show that coaching can enhance emotional intelligence, resilience, and leadership skills. For example, participants who underwent coaching reported better stress management and faster recovery from setbacks. Others found that coaching helped them develop empathy and make more thoughtful decisions—skills that influence many aspects of life.

Reflect on Buddha's journey once more. His transformation wasn't simply about meditating under a tree until clarity struck. It was a process of deep self-inquiry, questioning his beliefs, and reframing his understanding of the world. His enlightenment was the result of ongoing inner work, not a sudden moment of insight. Coaching mirrors this journey by guiding you to ask the questions that lead to your own kind of enlightenment—a clearer understanding of who you are, what you believe, and how you want to move forward.

The Art of Coaching

Coaching isn't about just asking any question; it's about asking the ones that dig deep and reveal what's truly beneath the surface. Two particularly effective techniques are "The Five Whys" and "Reframing Questions." These aren't mere methods; they're tools that help break through surface-level thinking and uncover the core of your beliefs and behaviors.

Take "The Five Whys," for instance. It's a simple but powerful tool where you repeatedly ask "why" to peel back the layers and get to the root of a problem or belief. While it might seem repetitive at first, each "why" moves you closer to understanding the real issue. You might start with, "I'm not good at public speaking." The first "why" might reveal a fear of judgment. The next might uncover a bad experience from the past. By the fifth "why," you could find a deep-seated belief about your self-worth that has nothing to do with speaking in public at all. This process doesn't merely address the symptoms; it tackles the root causes that hold you back.

Then there's "Reframing Questions." Instead of being stuck in a mindset of "Why can't I...?" shift the question to,

"What would it look like if I could…?" This subtle shift can make all the difference. Imagine feeling stuck in your career. Rather than focusing on limitations, you could ask, "What steps could I take to feel more fulfilled at work?" Suddenly, you're exploring opportunities instead of obstacles. It's about looking at the same situation from a new angle and realizing there are many ways to move forward.

These types of questions lead to moments of clarity—those instances when you suddenly see things differently, and in that shift, something changes. You recognize that the story you've been living isn't the only one available to you. One thoughtfully placed question can change your entire direction. It's not magic; it's a change in perspective.

Consider Sharan, a professional who felt lost in his career. By asking himself, "What if my job isn't the problem, but my approach to it is?" he opened up new possibilities. This single question led him to explore new roles within his company that better aligned with his values and strengths. A small change in the question led to a change in action, which altered his experience entirely. That's the power of asking the right questions.

However, these techniques only work in an environment of trust. Effective questioning and reframing happen best where you feel safe to explore. In a good coaching relationship, trust isn't based on authority; it's built on mutual respect. It's not about having all the answers or even giving perfect advice—it's about believing in the discovery process. A coach doesn't need to direct you; they walk alongside you, helping you see what you might have missed.

Trust allows for vulnerability. It creates a space where you can explore uncomfortable truths without fear of judgment. A mentor might share advice from their experience, and a therapist might help you understand your past, but coaching is different. It's focused on your present and future. It's about crafting an environment where you can explore your potential, guided but not directed. This balance of trust and respect sets the stage for real growth to happen.

Self-Coaching for Personal Mastery

Building a habit of self-coaching is about taking ownership of your own growth. It means regularly checking in with yourself, asking meaningful questions, and holding yourself accountable. Instead of relying on someone else to guide you, you become both the coach and the learner. It's about awareness, reflection, and taking intentional steps forward.

Begin by setting up weekly check-ins. Treat it as a meeting with yourself where you reflect on what you did last week, think about what worked and what didn't, and plan for the next week. During these check-ins, keep a reflection journal—a place to jot down thoughts, experiences, and insights. Writing things down can help you better understand your behavior and mindset, revealing patterns you might not notice otherwise.

Breaking down big goals into smaller, manageable tasks is another practical step. Instead of getting overwhelmed by long-term goals, set smaller, achievable steps. For instance, if you aim to improve at public speaking, start by practicing in front of a mirror for five minutes each day. These small, consistent actions build confidence and lead to bigger changes over time.

Learning to coach yourself is like developing any other skill; it requires consistent effort and a plan to stay on course. Reflecting on your experiences is crucial. After facing a challenging situation, take a moment to ask: "What did I learn? How could I have done better? What will I change next time?" These questions help turn every experience, good or bad, into an opportunity for growth. This practice is key to building resilience and continually improving.

Emotional intelligence is central to effective self-coaching. It's not just about knowing what you want; it's also about understanding your emotions and why you feel them. Developing emotional intelligence helps you manage your emotions in ways that support your goals rather than hinder them. Start by identifying your emotional triggers. Pay attention to when you have strong reactions—like anger, frustration, or anxiety. Ask yourself: "What caused this feeling? Was it something someone said? Did it remind me of something from the past?"

Managing these reactions constructively is the next step. Instead of responding impulsively, practice pausing. Take a deep breath, reflect on your options, and choose a response that aligns with your values and long-term goals. This small act of mindfulness can shift how you handle difficult situations, leading to better outcomes and stronger relationships.

Mastering self-coaching means understanding that life gives you as much as you ask for. But as the quote suggests, you must first deserve it—building both competence and character. This involves consistently working on yourself, honing your skills, and aligning your actions with your values. It's about earning the outcomes you desire by becoming the person who naturally achieves them.

By integrating these practices—self-reflection, setting micro-goals, and developing emotional intelligence—you create a framework for ongoing personal mastery. You're not waiting for life to give you direction; you're actively shaping your path, one thoughtful step at a time.

The journey to personal mastery isn't about following a predefined script; it's about writing your own story. It's a path shaped by the questions you ask, the choices you make, and the habits you build. Each day presents a new opportunity to grow, reflect, and take another step toward becoming the person you want to be. By becoming your own coach, you learn to lead yourself with intention, clarity, and purpose. And in doing so, you discover that the power to change your life is always within you, waiting to be tapped into. When you choose to engage fully, life responds in kind, opening doors you never knew existed. The journey of growth is continuous—one choice, one action, one step at a time.

Chapter 4

The Coaching Ripple

A young boy sat on the floor of his parent's garage, playing with electronics and exploring the wires and circuits sprawled around him. That boy was Steve Jobs, long before he became famous. He was curious and often felt out of place in school. While his classmates focused on grades and careers, Jobs wanted to understand how things worked and how to improve them. His adoptive father encouraged him to discover things for himself, to "figure things out on his own." This early support wasn't pushing him toward a specific path but helping him find his own way.

In many Indian households, kids face pressure to get perfect grades and choose "safe" careers. But imagine a different way. A child isn't pushed to memorize facts; they're asked why those facts matter. They learn to question, explore, and connect what they learn to the world around them. This approach isn't about being the smartest in the class. It prepares them for real-life challenges—thinking on their feet, solving problems, and handling setbacks.

Jobs hit a wall later in life—he got fired from Apple, the company he built. Instead of spiraling into regret, he used it as a chance to reflect. "What can I create next?" he asked, rather than "Why did this happen to me?" That shift—from being stuck on what went wrong to focusing on what's possible—can be a game-changer. It's not following a fixed path; it's finding your own, based on what drives you.

For many adults, life can feel like a series of checkboxes—graduate, find a job, get promoted. It's easy to end up in a role that looks good from the outside but drains you on the inside. A better question to consider isn't, "How can I earn more?" but, "What work makes me feel alive?" Jobs asked himself a similar question after his setback. When you change the question, the direction changes too. **It's not just about moving up the ladder but making sure the ladder is against the right wall.**

Later in his life, Jobs saw beyond just building products. His famous Stanford speech wasn't a call for success; it was a call for meaning. He talked about "connecting the dots," not by planning every step but by trusting each step as it came. This mirrors what reflection does, especially as life goes on. It guides you to consider, "What do I want to leave behind?" The focus shifts from counting accomplishments to finding what truly counts.

Jobs' journey shows that principles for growth aren't set in stone. They adapt. As a child, it's about curiosity. As an adult, it's about aligning actions with values. Later, it's about reflecting on what you've built and what really matters. The questions change, but the process stays the same—looking deeper, finding clarity, and making choices that feel right to you.

Growth isn't about achieving more. It's about living better.

Early Foundations - Building Mindsets from Childhood

Think back to your school days, where the focus was often on getting the most marks, memorizing answers, and following a set path. How often were you asked, "What did you learn today?" instead of, "How much did you score?" It's a subtle shift, but it changes everything. This question opens a door to curiosity, helping you connect what you learned to the world around you, rather than just another test paper.

In many Indian schools, children are taught to prioritize results over real understanding. But what if the emphasis was on learning to think, not just memorize? When a child is encouraged to ask why a math problem works a certain way or how a historical event shaped the present, they start to see beyond the textbook. They learn to challenge their thinking, explore new ideas, and build a sense of confidence in what they know, rather than fear of what they don't.

Coaching, in its simplest form, helps kids ask better questions—questions that go beyond just "Will this be on the test?" and into "How does this connect to what I see in the world?" This approach builds more than academic knowledge; it develops resilience, emotional awareness, and problem-solving skills. Think back to Steve Jobs' story - he wasn't the best student in the traditional sense, but he was deeply curious. He spent hours tinkering with electronics, not because it would get him good grades, but because he wanted to understand how things worked. That's how he developed his independent, unique way of thinking and a lifelong love of learning. Imagine a child not worried about a tough exam, but excited by the chance to learn something new, to stretch their understanding. This isn't just about grades; it's about preparing them for the challenges that lie ahead, both in school and in life.

Strategies for Children to Build Growth Mindsets:

- **Encourage Open-Ended Questions:** Focus on questions like "What if?" or "Why do you think this happens?" These stimulate curiosity and help them think critically about what they learn.

- **Create a Growth Environment at Home:** Avoid goals focused only on grades. Use phrases like, "I'm proud of how you handled that challenge" rather than "I'm proud you got an A." This mindset values effort and learning over just outcomes.

- **Use Real-World Applications:** Help children connect their studies with real-world situations. If they're learning about gravity, talk about how it affects everyday things like a cricket ball's trajectory or how a parachute works. This helps them see the relevance and apply their knowledge practically.

- **Promote Reflection:** After a task or challenge, ask, "What did you learn from this?" and "How could you approach it differently next time?" This encourages self-reflection, an essential part of growth, even at a young age.

Adulthood - Redefining Success Through Clarity and Reflection

As you move into adulthood, the questions evolve. The stakes are higher now. You're no longer just dealing with exams and grades but facing choices about your career, relationships, and personal growth. Many people, despite being successful by conventional standards, reach a point where they feel lost. The goals they worked so hard to achieve suddenly don't seem as satisfying.

This is where the idea of "deserve and then desire" becomes crucial. In adulthood, aspirations need to be backed by consistent effort and self-improvement. You can't just wish for a fulfilling career; you have to build it by aligning your actions with your values and working on yourself continuously. Jobs didn't just sit around after his setback. He co-founded Pixar and NeXT, continuing to push boundaries and challenge himself. His success wasn't about luck; it was about earning it through relentless effort and a clear vision.

At this stage, reflection helps shift the focus from external achievements to internal alignment. Instead of asking, "What's the next step up the career ladder?" a better question might be, "Does this work reflect who I am and what I want?" These are the questions that keep you grounded, guiding you to choices that feel true to you, not just to the expectations of others.

Steps for Adults to Find Meaning in Their Work and Lives

- **Regular Self-Check-ins:** At least once a month, take a step back to evaluate your personal and professional life. Ask yourself, "Am I where I want to be?" and "What adjustments do I need to make?"

- **Define Success on Your Terms:** Instead of adopting society's definition of success, define what it means to you. Is it about financial stability, creative freedom, meaningful relationships, or a combination of these?

- **SMART Goals with Flexibility:** While setting SMART goals, remain flexible. As you grow, your aspirations might change. Stay open to adjusting your goals as you gain more clarity.

Later Years - The Journey of Purpose and Legacy

As you approach the later stages of life, the questions take another turn. It's less about chasing new achievements and more about reflecting on the journey. "What did my life contribute?" and "What do I want to leave behind?" become the focus. Here, reflection isn't about pushing forward; it's about pausing to understand the story you've written and deciding how the final chapters will unfold.

For someone who spent decades building a career, retirement can feel like an abrupt stop. But it doesn't have to be. This stage is an opportunity to redirect your energy toward new, meaningful pursuits. It might mean mentoring others, engaging in community work, or even picking up a new passion.

Ways to Stay Engaged and Find Purpose:

- **Mentorship:** Share your knowledge with those just starting out. Your experience is valuable, and passing it on can bring a sense of fulfillment.

- **Join a Community:** Whether it's a hobby group or a volunteer organization, stay connected. It's not just about staying busy; it's about staying involved.

- **Lifelong Learning:** Commit to always learning. Read, explore, or take up new skills. Growth doesn't stop; it just changes form.

Transitions in life can feel like standing at a crossroads. You're not just choosing a path; you're deciding who you want to become. This is where the right questions and reflections come in. If we think back to Steve Jobs' story, we see these principles at work. After being ousted from Apple, he didn't just jump into the next venture. He took a moment to reflect deeply. What do I want to create? What impact do I want to leave? This was not just a reaction to failure but a deliberate choice to focus on what felt meaningful.

These pivotal moments come up for all of us—when you're considering a career change, thinking about retirement, or deciding on a new life direction. It's easy to get stuck on what others expect from you or on what seems safe. But the real work is in asking yourself what truly aligns with your values. When faced with a major life decision, think like Jobs: don't rush into the next big thing just because it's there. Pause, reflect, and ask yourself, "What do I want my life to look like next?" Sometimes, the answer isn't a leap; it's a pivot.

Educational Decisions and Personal Growth

Our choices in education and personal growth are some of the most significant decisions we make. These choices are not just about degrees or qualifications; they are about aligning with who we want to become. When you stand at these crossroads, it's easy to think in terms of what's practical. "What will give me the best salary?" is a question many ask. But a more meaningful question might be, "What will give me the most fulfillment?"

Take, for example, a young student named Aarav. This is a story of how coaching principles helped him navigate a challenging decision between pursuing a passion and choosing a safer career path. Aarav excelled in English literature. He loved writing—poetry, short stories, anything that allowed him to express himself creatively. But as his school years came to an end, the pressure began to mount. His family, like many, leaned towards safer career options. They suggested he consider an MBA in media management—a path that promised stability and financial security. While he didn't dislike the idea, something in him resisted. His love for literature and storytelling was strong, but it didn't seem "practical" in the eyes of others.

Aarav was torn. He could choose the path that was laid out for him, one that was considered safe, or he could follow his passion, even if it meant uncertainty. Instead of making a decision out of fear or pressure, he asked himself a simple yet powerful question: "Would I be happy doing this, even if it were challenging?" That clarity was a turning point. He realized that while an MBA could bring stability, it wouldn't bring him joy.

This was a difficult choice, but he made it by aligning with what felt true to him. He decided to pursue a degree in literature and creative writing, while also taking up a minor in digital media to have practical skills he could use alongside his passion. His decision wasn't about rejecting one path entirely; it was about blending his interests in a way that felt authentic.

Aarav's journey shows that when you're at a crossroads, the real question isn't which path is safer, but which path aligns with who you are. It's not enough to just set goals; they must be meaningful and rooted in what truly excites and challenges you.

Steps for Informed Decision-Making:

- **Clarify Your "Why":** Before making any big decision, ask yourself, "Why do I want this?" Take the time to write down your reasons. Are they driven by fear, expectation, or genuine passion? This clarity will help in staying committed when challenges inevitably arise.

- **Test the Waters:** Don't leap into a new field without some experience. Look for short-term projects, internships, or volunteer opportunities in that area. These experiences will give you a better understanding of what to expect and help you make a more informed choice.

- **Seek Honest Feedback:** Talk to people who have taken both paths—those who chose stability and those who followed their passion. Their stories, filled with real-life ups and downs, can provide perspectives that you won't find in any book or course.

Decisions like these aren't just choices; they're defining moments that shape your future. The right approach involves both reflection and action. You need the courage to take a step forward, but also the insight to ensure it's in the right direction.

The I Framework: Building Skills for Growth

As we move through different stages of life, it becomes clear that growth isn't just about knowing more or achieving more. It's about integrating the right set of skills that guide you through personal and professional challenges. This is where the I Framework comes into play—combining three key elements: Business Acumen, Technical Proficiency, and Interpersonal Skills. Together, these skills create a strong foundation for growth that isn't just narrow or specialized but well-rounded and adaptable.

Building Blocks for Success:

- **Business Acumen:** This is the ability to see the bigger picture, whether you're managing a business or making personal decisions. It's about understanding how choices lead to outcomes. Think of it as a way to see how different pieces fit together, helping you make informed decisions that create value, whether you're at work or managing your personal finances.

- **Technical Proficiency:** No matter the field, having specific skills sets you apart. Whether you're a coder, writer, or designer, being technically strong in what you do makes you effective. But it's not just about mastering

Elevating Human Intelligence

IT -Individual Transformation Framework

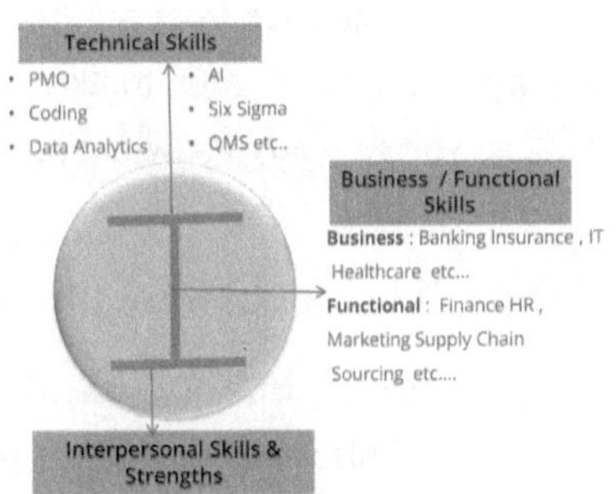

- Executive Communication
- Strategy
- Influencing
- Conflict Management
- Navigating

- Transformation / Change management
- Connecting the dots
- Brand Building / Executive Presence
- Courageous Leadership

a skill; it's about staying relevant, being open to learning, and applying those skills to solve real problems.

- **Interpersonal Skills:** Connecting with others, communicating clearly, and understanding different perspectives often determine how far you go. These skills are the bridge that connects your expertise to the world. Whether you're leading a team, negotiating a deal, or just building relationships, how you interact with people matters.

Bringing these three components together allows you to approach challenges from multiple angles. It's not just about having one tool in your toolkit; it's about having the right mix, so you're ready for whatever comes your way.

Putting the I Framework into Practice:

This framework isn't just an idea; it's practical. Consider how these skills work together in real life.

Rajat's Story: Shifting Mid-Career

Rajat was a marketing manager who was great with numbers and strategy (business acumen) but realized something was missing. He wasn't connecting well with his team and felt stuck. Instead of jumping to learn a new technical skill, he chose to work on his interpersonal skills. He started listening more, asking his team for input, and becoming more empathetic. This shift transformed his work environment. His team felt heard, and their performance improved. Rajat moved into a leadership role, not because he learned a new software tool, but because he learned to connect.

Steps to Apply the I Framework in Your Life:

- **Assess Where You Stand:** Take a moment to think about which areas you excel in and where you could grow. Are you great at your job but struggle to communicate your ideas? Or do you connect well with others but lack specific expertise?

- **Set Small, Clear Goals:** Focus on one area at a time. If you want to develop business acumen, start by reading a few key articles on strategy. If it's technical skills, take a short online course. For interpersonal skills, practice active listening in every conversation this week.

- **Get Real Feedback:** Ask those around you where they see your strengths and where you might improve. Sometimes an outside perspective is exactly what you need to see yourself clearly.

- **Reflect and Adapt:** Revisit your progress regularly. Are you finding that developing these skills is making a difference? Adjust your goals based on what you learn about yourself along the way.

Meera's Experience: Balancing Skills for Growth

Meera, a software developer, knew her technical skills were top-notch. But she also recognized that she wasn't always seeing the broader impact of her work or communicating effectively with her team. She decided to build her business understanding and improve her communication. She took courses on business strategy and participated in team-building exercises. Soon, she wasn't just contributing to projects—she was leading them.

By applying the I Framework, you're not just filling gaps. You're creating a strong, balanced approach to both life and career, ensuring that you're prepared for any challenge. It's about steady progress, where each skill complements the others, helping you grow not just in one direction but in all the ways that matter.

Reflecting on Steve Jobs' journey, you see a powerful example of the I Framework in action. Jobs blended business acumen, technical proficiency, and interpersonal insight throughout his life. He understood the market and created value with Apple and Pixar, showcasing his business sense. His technical brilliance shaped innovative products, but it was his ability to inspire and connect with people—whether it was his team, his customers, or the world at large—that truly set him apart. His story isn't just about building companies; it's about building himself. Each stage of his life was marked by a different focus, a different set of questions, and a different kind of growth. Just like Jobs, your journey is one of continuous learning, adapting, and integrating the skills that shape not just what you do, but who you become. Growth isn't static; it's a constant, active process of aligning your choices with your values, staying open to change, and crafting a life that feels genuinely yours.

PART 3

THE COACH APPROACH

Chapter 5

The Path to Purpose

A young girl sits in a classroom in Pakistan, surrounded by books and the sounds of children learning. She's just like any other child, excited to learn and dream about her future. But outside, the world is changing, and not for the better. There's tension in the air—a fear of losing the right to something as simple as education. This is Malala Yousafzai's story, but it could be anyone's—a story of finding purpose amidst adversity. When extremists tried to silence her voice, they unknowingly amplified it. She found her 'why'—to fight for every girl's right to learn. That purpose gave her clarity and courage, turning a schoolgirl into a global advocate. She wasn't just fighting for herself but for millions of girls like her who deserved to learn, to grow, and to be heard.

Think of purpose as the backbone of your life decisions. It isn't a vague feeling but a clear guiding principle that shapes your choices, motivates you through challenges, and gives your actions meaning. When you know your 'why,' every decision becomes more straightforward. You're no longer swayed by every new trend or opinion; you move with intention. Elon Musk, for example, doesn't just run companies—his 'why' drives him. He wants to advance sustainable energy and make space exploration possible for humanity's future. That purpose shapes everything from his business strategies to his daily routines. The clearer the purpose, the stronger the drive.

As Will Smith once said, "If you're not making someone else's life better, then you're wasting your time." Purpose doesn't have to be world-changing right away. It can start small—like making a difference in your community. Think about it: what's one small way you can positively impact someone's life this week? This isn't just an exercise in kindness; it's a step toward finding what truly matters to you.

When you have a clear 'why,' it guides you through both personal and professional decisions. It enhances your motivation and helps you stay resilient in the face of setbacks. Without a purpose, decisions can feel random or forced, like you're wandering without direction. But when you know why you're doing something, the path becomes clearer, and each step feels more intentional.

Ask yourself: Have you made a decision recently that felt out of sync with your true self? Maybe you chose a job that didn't align with your values or agreed to a project that didn't excite you. Reflect on that decision. If you had a clear purpose guiding you, would you have chosen differently?

Techniques to Identify Your Core Purpose

Finding your 'why' isn't always straightforward. It takes reflection and a bit of honesty. Here are a few ways to start:

1. **Values Alignment Checklist:** This is a simple tool to help you identify what truly matters. Ask yourself, "What would I stand up for, even if it were difficult?" or "What are the top three things I want to be known for?" When you align your actions with your values, you build a life that feels authentic and fulfilling.

2. **Purpose Audit:** Take a moment to conduct a 'Purpose Audit.' Reflect on your daily activities— are they moving you closer to your long-term goals? Or are they distractions pulling you away? Write down your answers. You might find that some routines or commitments no longer serve you.

3. **Purpose Journal:** Keep a journal dedicated to moments when you felt most alive or fulfilled. What were you doing? Who were you with? What made that moment special? Over time, patterns will emerge, showing you what truly resonates with your core. These insights are your clues to finding your 'why.'

Once you've identified your purpose, it becomes a filter for your decisions. Let's say you're deciding whether to take a new job. Instead of just looking at the salary or benefits, you ask, "Does this align with my long-term goals? Does it help me fulfill my purpose?" Suddenly, the decision isn't just about financial gain—it's about aligning with what feels meaningful.

Friedrich Nietzsche once said, "He who has a why to live can bear almost any how." When you're clear on your 'why,' the 'how' becomes more manageable. Think back to a challenging time in your life. Did you feel lost, unsure of which way to turn? Now, consider how a clearer sense of purpose could have provided direction. Reflect on that for a moment. How might things have been different?

From Stories to Actions:
Translating Purpose into Everyday Life

So, you've identified your 'why.' But what comes next? The stories of Malala and Musk are inspiring, but how do you take that inspiration and turn it into action? Here's where many people get stuck. They think living with purpose means making some grand change or finding a new life path overnight. But that's not how it works. Purpose isn't found in big, bold moves alone; it's built in the small, consistent steps you take every day.

Start simple. Look back at the values you identified in your alignment checklist. Pick one value that stands out to you—maybe it's integrity, creativity, or community. Now, think of a small way you can live that value this week. If you chose integrity, for instance, you might commit to being more honest in your conversations, even when it feels uncomfortable. If it's creativity, set aside 15 minutes each day to write, paint, or brainstorm new ideas. These actions don't have to be life-altering, but they do have to be intentional.

Consistency is where the magic happens. When you take small actions aligned with your purpose, you start to see a shift. It's not always immediate, but over time, these small choices compound, much like investing in a bank. The more consistently you live in line with your 'why,' the more you begin to feel aligned with your life.

Think of purpose as a muscle. It doesn't grow stronger by thinking about it or reading inspiring quotes—it grows through use. Just like going to the gym, the more you practice living by your values, the more natural it becomes. And the more natural it becomes, the clearer your path ahead looks.

Action Steps to Bring Purpose into Your Day-to-Day Life

1. **Pick a Value, Act on It:** Go back to your values alignment checklist. Pick one value and find one way to express it today. It doesn't need to be complex. If your value is 'community,' offer to help a neighbor or volunteer for a local cause. Small acts done consistently make a big impact over time.

2. **Create Micro-Habits Around Your Purpose:** Don't try to overhaul your life in one go. Instead, think of tiny, repeatable actions that reinforce your 'why.' If your purpose involves creativity, you don't need to write a novel in one sitting. Start with 10 minutes of free writing each morning. The goal is to make it so simple that it's hard to say no.

3. **Reflect Weekly:** Dedicate time at the end of each week to reflect on how well you lived by your values. Ask yourself, "Did I take at least one action each day that aligns with my purpose?" If not, what got in the way? This reflection isn't about guilt; it's about learning. The

more you understand what drives you or distracts you, the better you'll get at staying aligned.

4. **Build a Purpose Board:** Create a space—whether it's a physical board or a digital document—where you jot down quotes, images, and notes that connect to your purpose. Use it as a daily reminder of what you're working toward. The more you see it, the more it stays at the forefront of your mind.

5. **Celebrate Small Wins:** Recognize and celebrate when you live by your values, no matter how small the action. Did you stand up for what you believe in during a meeting? Celebrate that. Did you finally sign up for that course you've been meaning to take? Acknowledge that. These small moments reinforce the behavior you want to see more of.

Living with purpose doesn't mean your life will suddenly become easy. Challenges will still come, and there will be days when things don't go as planned. But when you have a clear 'why' and make small, purposeful choices every day, you start to build a life that feels genuinely yours. It's not about perfection—it's about direction. You don't have to see the whole path ahead; you just need to take the next step that aligns with your values. And then, keep going.

Overcoming Obstacles in the Path to Purpose

You've identified your 'why' and started to bring it into your everyday life. But what happens when the going gets tough? And it will. Finding and living your purpose doesn't mean the absence of obstacles; in fact, it often brings more challenges to the surface. The difference is in how you face them.

Everyone encounters roadblocks on the path to purpose. Fear of judgment, fear of failure, and societal pressures are just a few. Imagine being excited about a new career direction, only to have a friend or family member raise an eyebrow and say, "Are you sure that's a good idea?" Suddenly, the doubt creeps in. You start questioning yourself, not because you're unsure, but because someone else is.

There's a quote that hits this point well: "Doubt kills more dreams than failure ever will." Doubt makes you second-guess every decision, even the ones that felt so right initially. Think back to a time when you let doubt control your actions. Was it worth it? How did it feel to hold back on something that could have brought you closer to your purpose?

Building Resilience Through Purpose

When you have a clearly defined 'why,' it acts like a compass in stormy weather. It helps you stay on course when things get tough. Consider the story of J.K. Rowling, who faced numerous rejections before finally getting *Harry Potter* published. Her purpose wasn't just to write a book—it was to create a world that others could escape into, a story that could inspire and bring joy. When faced with rejection after rejection, she didn't give up. She realigned herself with her purpose and kept moving forward.

Here is how the resilient spirit of purpose helped another person find their way: When faced with the tough decision of leaving his stable corporate job to pursue social entrepreneurship, Arun found himself torn between financial security and his desire to create meaningful change. For months, he weighed the pros and cons, but it wasn't until he revisited his core purpose—his 'why' of wanting to empower underprivileged communities—that clarity emerged. Instead of being paralyzed by uncertainty, he focused on his deeper intention. This shift allowed him to take gradual steps, like volunteering part-time and networking within the social sector, before fully committing to his new path. His 'why' didn't just give him direction; it gave him the courage to act.

A well-defined purpose doesn't remove the obstacles; it simply makes them easier to face. It gives you a reason to get back up, to push through discomfort, and to keep going when things feel uncertain. Purpose becomes your anchor.

But how do you build this kind of resilience in your own life?

1. **Reframe Setbacks as Learning Opportunities:** Instead of seeing a setback as a failure, see it as a lesson. Ask yourself, "What can I learn from this? How can this help me grow?" This shift in perspective can turn any obstacle into a stepping stone.

2. **Create a Support Network:** Surround yourself with people who understand your 'why' and who encourage you to stay on your path. These are the people who will remind you why you started when doubt starts to creep in.

3. **Regular Self-Check-ins:** Just like you'd check a compass to make sure you're heading in the right

direction, take regular moments to check in with yourself. Are your actions still aligned with your values? If not, what needs to change?

Creating an Actionable Plan

Having a purpose isn't enough; you need a plan to bring it to life. It's like having a destination but no map. Start by creating a "Purpose Plan." Think of this as a practical guide to keep you aligned with your values and goals.

Here's How to Create Your Purpose Plan:

1. **Set Clear, Specific Actions:** Write down three to five actions that align with your purpose. Make them specific. Instead of saying, "Help my community," write, "Volunteer at the local food bank once a month." Clarity fuels action.

2. **Establish Checkpoints:** Every three months, revisit your plan. Reflect on what's working and what's not. Are there actions that have become more or less important? Adjust your plan accordingly.

3. **Stay Open to Change:** Purpose is not rigid; it's fluid. It grows and evolves with you. Be open to revising your plan as you gain new insights or as life circumstances change. Remember, the aim is not to stick to a plan blindly but to stay true to your values.

4. **Include Moments for Self-Reflection:** Make space in your schedule for regular reflection. Whether it's through journaling, talking with a mentor, or simply

taking a quiet walk, ensure there's time to think deeply about where you are and where you want to go.

Living a life aligned with purpose is a journey, not a destination. The road won't always be smooth, but with a well-defined 'why,' a supportive network, and a flexible plan, you can keep moving forward, no matter what comes your way.

Think back to the stories shared, whether it's Malala standing up for education, Musk driving toward sustainable innovation, or the everyday decisions that shape our own lives. Each of these stories started with a clear 'why.' And that 'why' became the anchor that grounded them through the waves of uncertainty, challenge, and doubt. It wasn't just a moment of inspiration—it was a continual, evolving commitment to a path that felt true to them.

Living with purpose isn't a one-time decision. It's a series of choices you make every day. It's choosing the work that aligns with your values, even when the easier path promises more immediate rewards. It's deciding to take small, meaningful steps rather than waiting for a big, transformative moment. Your 'why' can evolve, just as you do.

Take a Step Today: Ask yourself one simple question: "What is one small thing I can do this week that aligns with my values?" It could be as simple as reaching out to someone in need, starting a journal to reflect on what truly matters, or just taking five minutes every morning to remind yourself of your core 'why.' Small actions create momentum, and that momentum can lead to significant change.

Remember, your purpose is not a destination; it's a journey. There will be times when the road isn't clear when doubt or fear tries to pull you off course. But this is where your 'why' comes in—your anchor. It doesn't mean the challenges disappear, but it gives you something solid to hold on to when the winds are strong.

Chapter 6

Your World Inside Out

Life doesn't move in a straight line; it flows through a series of circles that represent different stages. Think of these circles as phases we move through: being a student, entering the workforce, progressing into mid-level roles, and eventually stepping into leadership positions. Each stage comes with its own challenges and opportunities. This idea of "Life in Circles" shows that growth isn't linear; it's an ongoing journey where expanding your skills, mindset, and resilience matters.

Imagine these circles as layers in a tree trunk. Each layer represents growth over time. As you grow, you move through these circles—sometimes standing between two, like transitioning from student life to your first job or from mid-level to senior positions. At every stage, there's a learning curve. To navigate these shifts smoothly, continuous learning becomes essential.

For instance, the first circle spans the ages of 18-22, typically when you're a student. It's the stage where gaining skills, exploring different interests, and seeking real-world

Life in Circles

Transitioning	Students	Entry level jobs	Pre / Mid level job	Senior level job	CXO level job
Professional Life					
Typical age group	18 -22	23 -27	28 -35/40	36 -45/50	45 -50+
Coaching Interventions	TDP : Talent Discovery Program	CAP : Corporate Acceleration Program	LAP : Leadership Acceleration Program	TLP : Transformation Leadership Program	SLP : Strategic Leadership Program

For this journey of elevation one needs to continuously go through IT – Individual Transformation at every stage of life

---

Life in Circles

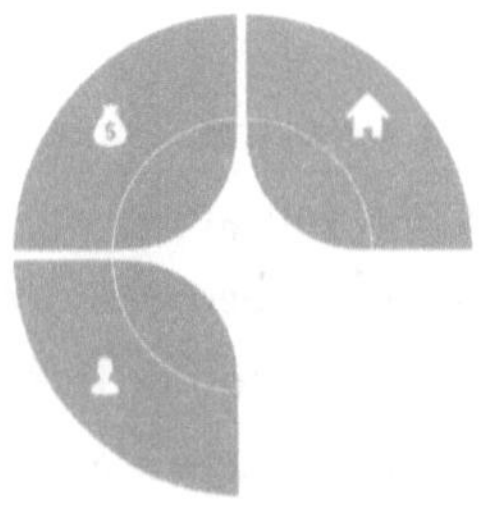

Giftt : Helping in addressing two critical questions on people's mind :

01. What Next ?

At every stage of our life right from students' stage through professional career, this question of "**what next**" pops up in everyone's mind

02. How Next ?

We at GIFTT help you in finding how to take right path through scientific assessments and exposure

How do you prepare for your next ?

The Question to ask yourself is are your preparing for this journey and how ?

experiences through internships or projects help you prepare for what's next. The second circle, covering ages 23-27, involves entry-level roles where adaptability and learning on the job are key as industries evolve and trends shift.

As you move into the 28-35/40 age range, the pre- or mid-level job stage, the expectations grow. It's no longer just about technical skills; leadership abilities and strategic thinking become central as your influence expands. The following circle, around ages 36-45/50, involves senior roles where guiding teams, managing projects, and mentoring others take priority. Finally, the CXO level, typically for ages 45 and above, involves broader responsibilities where the impact of your decisions reaches wider circles.

These transitions show that moving from one stage to another is not passive—it requires an active effort. Whether it's building skills, investing in relationships, or expanding your perspective, these actions help you grow through each circle. Questions like "What's next?" or "How do I prepare for it?" guide each phase, ensuring you're equipped for the transitions ahead.

But while it's easy to get caught up in these external markers—titles, achievements, and expectations—what truly shapes your experience in each stage is your inner world. The "Life in Circles" concept connects the outer journey with your internal state. How you handle each transition, the choices you make, and the growth you experience depend on your inner strength and mindset. Understanding this connection between your inner and outer worlds sets the stage for balancing both and finding fulfillment.

While you move through these stages, it's not only the external progress that matters; the internal experience shapes how you move forward and grow within each circle.

Balancing the Circles

Ever have one of those days when everything looks fine on the surface, but inside, you're just trying to keep it together? Maybe you're at work, delivering presentations, answering emails, keeping up the rhythm, but there's a storm brewing in your mind. You smile at colleagues, nod through meetings, but your thoughts are elsewhere—replaying a difficult conversation, worrying about an unresolved issue, or feeling the weight of expectations. On the outside, you're composed; on the inside, you're anything but. This disconnect between the outer world people see and the inner world only you know is more common than you think.

Our lives often feel like a juggling act between what's happening outside—career goals, societal expectations, cultural norms—and what's happening inside—our emotions, thoughts, and mental well-being. The two worlds are closely linked. A rough day at work can stir up frustration that seeps into your time at home. Similarly, a personal conflict can make every task at work feel heavier. Most of us put energy into managing the external world—chasing achievements, fulfilling roles, meeting expectations—but how often do we check in on our inner world?

Think about a high-achieving student, for example. On paper, they're doing everything right: top grades, extracurricular activities, accolades from teachers. But inside, they're anxious and overwhelmed, struggling to keep pace with the pressure. Or think of a professional whose career graph is on the rise. They're hitting their targets and receiving praise, yet they feel disconnected, exhausted by the constant grind. Or think about your favorite Instagram influencers, who always seem put together and live picture-perfect lives, but are secretly struggling with their own issues, insecurities, and anxieties. These examples aren't stories—they're real-life reminders that success outside doesn't always mean peace inside.

Recognizing the Power of the Inner World

In the earlier chapters, we talked about the four pillars that define what life is all about—experiences, relationships, continuous learning, and emotions. Here, emotions take center stage. They are not just one of the pillars; they form the bedrock of our inner world. Your emotions shape how you interpret the world, how you interact with others, and how you handle challenges. They are the unseen force that can either fuel growth or hold you back.

Your inner world is the silent driver behind every choice you make, every action you take. Research shows that mental and emotional health isn't just an added benefit—it's the foundation. A calm and centered mind helps you make better decisions, handle setbacks more gracefully, and connect more deeply with others. On the flip side, when your inner world is chaotic, even small problems can feel overwhelming. The energy you spend managing internal stress leaves less for the things that truly matter.

Think back to a recent time when you felt stressed or anxious. How did it affect your day? Did you avoid an important conversation, miss a chance to try something new, or react harshly to a loved one? These reactions often stem from an inner world that needs attention. Recognizing these moments is the first step to finding balance. As we've discussed, emotions are not just passing feelings; they are indicators, guiding us toward what needs care and attention.

Balancing these two worlds doesn't mean everything is always in perfect harmony. It means knowing where your energy goes, understanding what fuels your inner peace, and choosing actions that keep you aligned. It's like tending to both the soil and the weather in a garden—one feeds the other, creating a space where growth happens naturally. When you invest in both, you build a life that feels grounded and real, where the outside reflects the inside.

Cultivating Inner Harmony

Recognizing the power of the inner world is just the beginning. The next step is to cultivate it, to actively manage what goes on inside so that it serves you rather than works against you. Just like tending to a garden, where you must water the plants, prune the branches, and pull out the weeds, your inner world requires regular attention and care. The goal isn't to erase all stress or never feel anxious—it's to learn how to respond to those feelings in ways that keep you centered.

Techniques for Managing the Inner World

1. Mindfulness and Meditation

Think of mindfulness as hitting a pause button in the middle of a busy day. It's not about emptying your mind or reaching some lofty spiritual goal; it's about bringing your focus back to the present moment. When you're mindful, you notice the small things—your breath, the sound of the leaves rustling, the warmth of the sun on your face. These moments pull you away from the spiral of stress or overthinking and ground you in the now.

Try a simple meditation technique: sit comfortably, close your eyes, and take a few deep breaths. Focus on the sensation of the breath entering and leaving your body. If your mind starts wandering, gently bring it back to the breath. Start with just five minutes a day. This practice isn't about achieving perfect calm but about building the habit of returning to the present whenever you need to.

2. Emotional Journaling

Journaling can be like having a conversation with yourself. It's a way to lay out your thoughts, understand your emotions, and see patterns that you might not notice in the busyness of daily life. When you write down your feelings, you start to see what triggers them—whether it's a particular person, situation, or even a specific time of day.

Begin with these prompts: "What emotion did I feel today and why?" or "How did my emotions influence my actions today?" Writing these down helps you recognize which emotions tend to dominate your day and which ones you want to cultivate more of. Over time, this self-awareness becomes a tool you can use to guide your choices and actions more deliberately.

3. Cognitive Behavioral Strategies

Sometimes, the way we think is what gets us stuck. Cognitive Behavioral Techniques (CBT) offer simple but effective ways to change those thought patterns. One method is to challenge negative thoughts and replace them with more balanced ones. For example, if you catch yourself thinking, "I always mess up," ask, "Is that really true?" Then, think of instances where you succeeded. This reframing isn't about being unrealistically positive; it's about seeing things as they are—not worse than they are.

Another powerful strategy is practicing gratitude. Take a moment each day to jot down three things you're grateful for. They don't have to be big—maybe it's the taste of your morning coffee or a call from a friend. Gratitude shifts your focus from what's lacking to what's already good in your life, subtly reshaping your emotional landscape.

4. Actionable Steps for Inner Stability

As Buddha wisely put it, "The mind is everything; what you think, you become." If your thoughts are rooted in negativity or fear, that's the reality you create. But if you cultivate a mindset of growth, gratitude, and calm, your external world begins to reflect that.

Here's how you can start: pick one or two techniques from above—whether it's mindfulness, journaling, or cognitive strategies—and make them a part of your daily or weekly routine. Keep it simple. Set aside ten minutes in the morning for mindfulness or dedicate five minutes before bed for journaling. The aim is consistency, not perfection.

Creating a Stable Internal Environment

Building a stable internal environment doesn't mean eliminating stress or avoiding challenges. It's about learning to respond in ways that keep you grounded. Stress will come, challenges will arise, but they don't have to derail you. Instead, think of them as waves in the ocean—inevitable but manageable. You can't control the waves, but you can learn to surf.

Consider the story of Meera, a software developer who was known for her sharp skills but struggled with self-doubt and anxiety. Whenever deadlines loomed or conflicts arose, she would feel overwhelmed. She decided to introduce mindfulness into her daily routine and committed to journaling her thoughts each night. Over time, she noticed a shift. She wasn't immune to stress, but she became better at recognizing when it was creeping in and responding before it took over. Her internal world became more stable, and as a result, her external reality improved—better focus at work, healthier relationships, and a greater sense of well-being.

Remember, stability inside doesn't come from the absence of difficulty; it comes from practicing how to remain steady when difficulty appears.

Engaging with the External World

The work of nurturing your inner world lays the foundation, but there's another layer to consider—the outer world. The world around you doesn't operate in a vacuum. It's filled with societal expectations, cultural norms, and economic realities that all have a say in the choices you make. Often, these influences can pull you away from what you truly want, guiding you to a place that might look successful on the outside but feels empty inside.

Understanding External Influences

Think of Nikhil, a bright student who excelled in science and math. His family always envisioned him becoming a doctor, a career seen as respectable and financially stable. Nikhil was good at it—his grades showed promise. But his passion lay elsewhere; he had always been fascinated by literature and dreamed of becoming a writer. Yet, the societal pressure to follow a "secure" path weighed heavily on him. He found himself at a crossroads, torn between following his heart and meeting the expectations placed upon him.

This is a common struggle. From career choices to personal relationships, external influences often shape our decisions more than we realize. We're taught to measure success by external standards—status, income, or societal approval. But what happens when these standards don't align with who you are?

To understand where these influences come from and how they affect you, take a moment to assess. Are your decisions being driven by what you truly value, or by what you think will gain the most approval? Are you pursuing a path because it's what you want, or because it's what others expect?

Strategies for Aligning Values with Actions

Once you recognize these influences, the next step is to align your actions with your inner values. It starts with clarity. Knowing what matters most to you becomes your anchor, especially when the external world tries to pull you in different directions.

1. Creating a Values-Based Decision Framework

Think of this as your personal filter for making choices. Before making a big decision—whether it's a job offer, a major purchase, or a relationship commitment—run it through your "Values Check." Ask yourself: "Does this align with my core values?" "Will this bring me closer to the person I want to become?" By doing this, you ensure that your actions are not just reactions to external pressures but intentional steps that resonate with who you are.

2. Choosing Supportive Environments

Jim Rohn famously said, "You are the average of the five people you spend the most time with." Take a look at your surroundings—your friends, colleagues, even your family. Are these people lifting you up, or are they keeping you stuck? It doesn't mean cutting ties with everyone who disagrees with you, but it does mean being mindful of who influences your mindset and actions.

Start by identifying communities or groups that share your values and goals. This could be a professional network, a hobby club, or even an online community. Surrounding yourself with people who understand and support your journey can make a world of difference. If you're looking to grow, find those who challenge and inspire you, rather than those who keep you in your comfort zone.

3. Action Plan for Engaging with the External World

Now, let's turn these insights into action. Here's a step-by-step approach to aligning your outer world with your inner values:

- **Set Boundaries**: Start small. Decide which areas of your life need boundaries—work, family, social circles—and set clear limits. This could mean saying no to extra work that doesn't add value to your career or politely declining a social event that drains your energy.

- **Seek Growth Environments**: Identify one new environment that aligns with your values. This could be a new gym where people focus on overall well-being rather than just aesthetics, or a professional group where members support rather than compete with each other.

- **Intentional Choices**: Before committing to anything—big or small—pause and ask, "Is this a reflection of my inner values?" Whether it's deciding how to spend your weekend or choosing a new job role, let this question guide you.

The goal isn't to eliminate all external influences—they're an inevitable part of life. It's to choose which ones serve you and to consciously build an environment that supports your journey.

Life is often a dance between what happens inside us—our thoughts, emotions, values—and what happens around us—the expectations, demands, and circumstances that shape our daily lives. When one is out of sync with the other, that's when imbalance creeps in. The key is not to shut out the world or be swayed entirely by it but to learn how to harmonize the two.

Think of it as a rhythm you create, where the inner world sets the beat and the outer world brings the melody. Both are needed to create a tune that feels right, a life that feels balanced and fulfilling. This balance doesn't mean there won't be times of dissonance. There will be days when the external demands are loud, and the internal calm feels out of reach. But the more you practice integrating these worlds, the easier it becomes to find your way back to the rhythm that works for you.

Choose Your Focus This Week

Let's put this into practice. This week, choose one area to focus on—your inner world or your outer world. If you find that your inner peace is often disturbed, maybe it's time to introduce a few minutes of mindfulness or journaling into your daily routine. If you feel pulled in too many directions by external pressures, take a step back and evaluate which influences serve you and which ones need boundaries.

Take One Small Step: Pick one small, actionable step from this chapter and commit to it for a week. If it's nurturing your inner world, perhaps start with a morning meditation or a daily gratitude journal. If it's engaging more intentionally with the outer world, maybe reassess the environments you spend most of your time in or have a conversation that's been on your mind. Remember, the goal is not to perfect the balance but to practice it, to keep moving closer to a life that feels aligned both inside and out.

Chapter 7

From Comparison to Aspiration: Your New Mantra

Think about the time when you thought you were living someone else's life. Maybe you're sitting here in this conference room, nodding, but your head is somewhere else. You glance at your coworker across the table; it seems everything in life is going right for them. They always seem to be one step ahead, getting the promotions, the praise, and the corner office. It feels like their LinkedIn profile is just a list of achievements, and every time they succeed, it seems like they're getting further ahead of you. You start to wonder, "What am I doing wrong?"

This was what it felt like to be Kunal. He was doing everything that should have brought satisfaction—working hard, hitting his targets, collecting kudos. But it was never enough. The more he looked around, the more others seemed to be doing better: one had a bigger house, another had already climbed the ladder to a higher position, and then there were those whose social media feeds seemed like the highlight reel of some sort of perfect life—exotic vacations, flawless families, dream jobs. Instead of being inspired, though, he felt drained, caught in the loop of never quite measuring up.

If you've ever felt like Kunal, you're not alone. We all do it—looking at someone's social media, seeing a successful friend, or watching a coworker advance quicker than we are. It's easy to compare ourselves to others. While this feeling is normal, it can often make us feel worse instead of better.

Understanding the Trap of Constant Comparison

We're naturally inclined to compare ourselves to others. This instinct was once useful—it helped our ancestors learn important skills for survival. But in today's world, this instinct can often do more harm than good. Instead of helping us move ahead, it can make us feel unsure and frustrated..

Think about a time you compared your life to someone else's. Was it a friend whose career seemed to take off, making you question your own path? Or maybe a stranger's perfect life on Instagram that made you feel stuck? These moments usually don't help us grow; they often make us feel like we're not good enough.

Why does this happen so often? Feeling unsure of ourselves and doubting our potential is common, and it connects to how our world works. Social media shows the best moments of others in their highlight reels—like their successes and happy times—but it rarely shows their 'behind the scenes' or struggles. The same happens at work. Reviews and promotions can make us feel like we are always competing, as if there is a limited amount of success. We often measure our worth by job titles, possessions, and achievements, but true happiness doesn't come from those things.

Remember: "Comparing yourself to others steals your happiness."Every time you pay attention to someone else's life, you miss what's happening in your own. Remember a time when you compared yourself to someone and felt down? Maybe it was when you saw a friend succeed and began to doubt your own choices? Or maybe it was seeing a perfect relationship online while dealing with your own ups and downs? Instead of giving in to doubt, think about where you are and where you want to go. If you catch yourself comparing to others, take a moment to ask, "Does this help me improve, or does it just make me feel bad?" Changing your perspective like this can really help. It's about finding your own path and shining in your own way.

Strategies for Focusing on Personal Aspirations

You've probably felt it before—constantly checking what others are doing and feeling like you're not keeping up. It's a common struggle. But what if you stopped comparing yourself to others and started setting your own goals? Think about creating a way to track your personal growth, focusing on who you're becoming rather than what others have done. This change—from looking at others to focusing on yourself—is where real change happens.

Start by thinking about what success means to you. People often say you should go after job titles, money, or status, but real success is about who you are becoming while you try to reach your goals. What if, instead of chasing what seems good from the outside, you focused on what really matters to you? What if, for once in your life you let go of the idea of *"log kya kahenge"* ("what will people say?")?

Make a "Personal Growth Chart" to track how you're doing with your goals and values. Think of it as a map that shows important steps in your journey. Instead of chasing a job title, focus on learning new skills, making better friends, or being more creative at work or in your community. These little wins might not get likes on social media, but they can bring you a lot of happiness.

Exercise: Creating Your Personal Growth Chart

1. **Identify Key Areas of Growth:** Think of areas that matter to you—career, health, relationships, personal development. List them out.

2. **Set Your Benchmarks:** Under each area, write down specific goals that align with your values. These should be measurable but personal to you—like "read 10 books on personal growth this year" or "dedicate 30 minutes a day to learning a new language."

3. **Track Your Progress:** At the end of each week or month, check in with yourself. Are you moving closer to these goals? What can you adjust? Remember, this isn't about perfection but progress.

While you work on your chart, remember this quote: "Success isn't about what you have, but who you are becoming." Think about what success means to you. Is it about hitting a goal, or is it more about the growth and lessons you learn on the journey? Define success in your own way to help you stay focused on your path.

Redirecting Energy from Comparison to Aspiration

When you stop looking at what others are doing and pay attention to your own progress, everything shifts. Instead of feeling jealous or doubtful, use that energy to cheer yourself on and take steps forward. When someone else does well, think of it as proof that you can do great things too. Learn from their story, but remember to stay focused on your own journey.

It's essential to remember that being successful matters more than appearing successful. In a world where everyone shares their highlights, it's easy to feel the need to keep up appearances. But true success comes from genuinely reaching your goals and finding fulfillment, not from what others see. Having real wealth holds more value than simply looking wealthy—what you truly achieve always counts more than what's perceived.

Think of a time when you felt really inspired to chase a new goal, like starting a business, writing a book, or running a marathon. At first, you were really excited, but then that excitement faded and the goal seemed too big. Many people give up right at the start. The difference between those who dream and those who reach their goals is often one thing: taking action.

Look at Rohan's journey. He wanted to leave his stable corporate job to start his own social enterprise. The idea excited him but also felt overwhelming. Instead of feeling stuck, he broke his big dream into small, easy steps. First, he focused on networking and meeting people in the field. Then, he spent his weekends learning the basics of business management and funding. He didn't rush to the finish line; he started small but took action. "Dream big. Start small. But most of all, start." His journey was not only about making one big leap; it was about taking the first step and then the next one.

To reach any goal, break it into smaller steps. Use SMART goals: Specific, Measurable, Achievable, Relevant, and Time-bound. For example, instead of saying "finish a book" in a month, say "write 500 words a day for 30 days." Taking small and clear steps helps you stay focused and keep going. The most successful people aren't always the most talented; they are the ones who keep taking action.

It's great to set goals and take action, but remember, the main thing is to make a difference, not to compete with others. Comparing yourself to someone else can pull you away from your own path and make you chase things that aren't meant for you. What works for one person might not work for you. We all have our own strengths, and getting better starts with knowing that. Focus on improving yourself—whether that's being a better worker, a nicer friend, or a happier person. This will help you move forward in ways that comparing yourself to others never will.

In life, there will always be people who compare themselves to you or others. That's okay. Instead, focus on your own goals. Aim to make a positive impact—whether it's on the people around you, the work you do, or your community. Remember, the right goals can motivate you, while the wrong ones can hold you back. So, choose your goals wisely. Make sure they match who you are and the difference you want to make.

Building Resilience and Perseverance

Aspirations can be challenging and often come with difficulties. The key is to keep pushing forward, even when things get hard. Take Murlikant Petkar, for instance. He was an Indian soldier who was badly injured in the 1965 India-Pakistan war and became paralyzed from the waist down. While many might see this as the end of his sports dreams, for Petkar, it was just the beginning of a new journey.

Even though he was in a wheelchair, Petkar didn't give up. Instead, he focused on swimming, a sport he had never tried professionally before. With hard work and determination, he trained himself against all odds. In 1972, he went to the Paralympics in Heidelberg, Germany, where he not only competed but also won India's first gold medal in swimming, setting a world record in the 50-meter freestyle.

Petkar's journey wasn't a straight path. He faced many setbacks and challenges, but he kept going, taking it one small step at a time. His story reminds us that being strong isn't just about bouncing back; it's about moving forward—turning difficulties into chances for a better comeback. When things get tough, think of Petkar's example as a reminder that struggles don't mean you're failing; they mean you're getting ready for something better. Keep dreaming and keep pushing on.

Our ability to imagine a better version of ourselves or a better world is one of our greatest gifts. It helps us start on a path, even if it's not clear, toward something good. This is where resilience comes in. When challenges pull us back, like an arrow being pulled, it often means we're getting ready to move forward. Facing challenges doesn't mean you're going off track; it means you're preparing to rise higher.

Being resilient isn't just about getting through tough times; it's about using those tough times to grow. When you hit obstacles, take a moment to think about them. Ask yourself, "What can I learn from this?" or "How can I handle this better next time?" Remember, it's not the setback that defines you, but how you choose to move ahead.

Action Steps for Staying Motivated

To stay on track, build a personal support system. This could be a vision board to remind you of your reasons, a friend who checks in on your progress, or a small group with similar goals. Positive affirmations are also helpful. They might seem simple, but they remind you daily of what you can do. Start your day with a saying like, "I can achieve my goals, one step at a time."

Try the "Weekly Win" challenge. At the end of each week, try jotting down just one thing you did to get closer to your goal, no matter how tiny it seems. It could be asking someone for advice, reading a chapter of a book, or even just taking a moment to unwind. When you focus on these little wins, you start to see your progress instead of stressing about perfection. Remember, those small steps can lead to some big changes!

When we start comparing ourselves to others, we end up missing the joy of our own journey. It's like running a race with a finish line that keeps moving—there's no peace or happiness, just a feeling of constant exhaustion. So, be real about where you are and clear about what you want. Take small steps every day, and let those steps come from your own dreams, not what everyone else is doing.

Here's a little challenge for you: Choose one personal goal for the next month that truly matters to you—something you genuinely desire, rather than just an obligation or trend you feel compelled to follow because others are doing it. Take a moment to reflect on what sparks joy or fulfillment in your life, and write that goal down!

Once you've got it all written down, try to take one tiny step toward that goal every day. It could be as simple as spending a few minutes reading that book you've been excited about, setting aside time to practice a new skill—like playing an instrument or learning a new language—or even reaching out to someone who inspires you, like a mentor or a friend who shares your interests.

Keep a small journal or a note on your phone to track your progress. Don't stress over what others are doing; concentrate on your own journey. By the end of the month, you'll feel more purposeful, have a clearer direction, and feel more in touch with the person you are growing into. Remember, it's not so much what you have; it's who you're becoming.

Start today. Your journey from comparing yourself to others to aiming for your own goals begins now.

Chapter 8

Formula for Success: Knowledge Meets Confidence

Unpacking the Formula: Knowledge + Confidence

"Whether you think you can,
or you think you can't—you're right."

– Henry Ford

How many times have you held back an idea because you weren't sure it was good enough? How often did you stay quiet in a meeting even though you knew the answer, just because you doubted yourself? And, how many times did you refrain from raising your hand in class, only to have someone else say the same answer you were thinking of? Confidence, or the lack of it, can be what keeps us stuck or helps us move forward.

Sundar Pichai, the CEO of Google, experienced this struggle early in his career. What made him stand out wasn't just his tech skills; it was his belief in his ideas when others didn't see the vision. He didn't wait for approval from others; he trusted himself and had confidence in his ability to make things happen on his own.

When he was starting out, Pichai had a big, bold idea: to build a new web browser. When he first introduced Google Chrome, not everyone was on board. Many people thought it was unnecessary and questioned if we really needed another browser. But Pichai believed in his vision. With the technical skills to support his idea and the confidence to pursue it, he turned Google Chrome into the most popular web browser today. This story isn't just a success tale; it reminds us that having knowledge isn't enough. Without confidence, even the best ideas may never come to life.

Knowledge is really important; it gives us the tools we need to succeed. It shows us what to do and how to do it. But without confidence, that knowledge can just sit there. Confidence helps you take that first step and make choices when others hesitate. It pushes you forward, even when things are uncertain.

Think of it this way: you could be the best chess player, knowing all the right moves. But if you're too afraid to make a single move, that knowledge won't do you any good. It's having the confidence to trust your instincts and act on what you know that really matters.

Why Knowledge Alone Isn't Enough

You might have all the information you need to succeed, but if you don't believe in yourself, that knowledge can actually hold you back. Have you ever felt like you knew what to do but something stopped you? That "something" is often a lack of confidence. It's like knowing the rules of a game but not actually playing it because you're shy.

Think back to a time when you had good ideas but didn't speak up because you weren't sure of yourself. Maybe it was at work when you had a great suggestion but remained silent, or in your personal life when you knew the right choice but hesitated and held back. How would things have changed if you had trusted yourself? We often miss out on opportunities not because we don't know enough, but because we doubt our ability to succeed.

Confidence is more than just feeling good about yourself. It's believing you can handle challenges, even when you don't have all the answers. It helps you grab opportunities, learn from mistakes, and keep going when things get tough. For instance, Sundar Pichai wasn't sure Chrome would succeed, but he trusted himself to learn, adapt, and make it work.

Confidence is what turns your knowledge into action. It lets you take that first step, even if the way forward feels unclear. When you're confident, you trust your own choices instead of waiting for others to approve, even when people doubt you.

Actionable Steps for Building Confidence

Building confidence takes time; it doesn't happen overnight. It's a journey that requires patience and effort. You can start boosting your confidence step by step by adding a few simple habits to your daily routine. Over time, these habits can help you feel better and give you the strength to face challenges with more confidence.

Techniques for Cultivating a Healthy Self-Belief System

Small Wins Build Big Confidence

Start small. Remember the first time you rode a bike or gave a presentation? It probably didn't feel great at first. But with practice, you got better. Confidence is similar. You don't need to make a huge leap to prove yourself; you just need a small win—something that tells you, "Hey, I can do this." Over time, these little wins build up and create a strong base for tackling bigger challenges.

Whether it's raising your hand in a meeting, sharing a new idea with your team, or trying something new, every small step helps you gain momentum.

In the workplace, you often see people with a lot of knowledge who are too shy to share their ideas. Without the confidence to speak up, their contributions stay hidden. That's why it's important to build your confidence along with your knowledge. After all, if you don't show what you can do, no one will know what you're capable of.

Self-Talk and Mindset Shifts

We all talk to ourselves, and sometimes that talk can be pretty negative. You might find yourself thinking, "I can't do this" or "I'll probably mess up." Does that sound familiar?

Now, imagine turning that around and being your own biggest supporter. Positive self-talk can really change how you feel. Instead of saying, "I'm not good enough," try telling yourself, "I'm learning, and I'll get better." It's a small change, but it can make a big difference.

Even saying simple things like "I am capable" or "I can handle challenges" can really help. Start by writing down something nice you say to yourself each morning, and you'll notice the effects over time.

And remember: "Confidence doesn't come from always being right, but from being okay with being wrong." It's perfectly fine not to have all the answers. Confidence grows when you're willing to try new things, even if they feel a bit uncertain.

Exposure to Discomfort

Confidence grows when you tackle uncomfortable situations. Remember the first time you tried something new? It was probably awkward and scary. But by the third or fourth try, it started to feel easier. That's because confidence comes from practice. The more you step outside your comfort zone, the more at ease you become.

Whether it's sharing your thoughts in a group, trying something new at work, or taking on a big challenge, every time you face discomfort, you build your confidence. When tough times hit, think of the eagle. Eagles don't shy away from storms; they soar above them, using the wind to rise higher. Just like that, you can turn discomfort into a way to lift yourself up, too.

Create a Confidence Ladder

Think of your confidence like a ladder. To reach the top, you have to take that first step. Write down the areas where you want to grow, like speaking up more in meetings or picking up a new skill. Then, break it down into smaller steps. If public speaking is your goal, start by sharing a quick idea in a small meeting. Once you feel good about that, keep climbing—maybe lead a project or present to a larger group. Each step builds on the one before, and soon you'll find yourself reaching heights you never imagined.

Reflect on Past Successes

It's easy to overlook your accomplishments, especially when self-doubt creeps in. That's why keeping a "Success Journal" can really help. Whenever you achieve something, no matter how small, jot it down. Finished a tough project? Write it down. Got through a challenging situation? Add it to your list. When you're feeling unsure or lacking confidence, take a moment to flip through your journal and remember all the wins you've had. Every little victory matters.

Seek Constructive Feedback

Feedback can feel a bit scary, but it's actually one of the best ways to grow. The key is to ask the right people—mentors, friends, or colleagues who genuinely want to see you succeed. They'll highlight what you're doing well and where you can improve, not to bring you down, but to help you rise.

Remember, feedback isn't about pointing out flaws; it's a guide to help you get better.

The Knowledge-Confidence Synergy

Knowledge and confidence go hand in hand; they're closely connected. You can see this in the stories of people who have made a real difference by not only understanding their field but also believing in themselves enough to take bold steps.

Take Sundar Pichai, for example. He showed how knowing the tech world and having the confidence to push for his idea for Google Chrome made a huge impact, even when others weren't sure a new browser was needed. But his journey didn't end there. Every part of his career, from leading Chrome to becoming Google's CEO, was all about knowing his stuff and having the guts to make things happen.

What's key here is how his confidence grew alongside his knowledge. Early in his career, Sundar wasn't leading a global tech giant. He was like any of us—learning, growing, and taking small steps. With each project he led, he gained more experience, which in turn fueled his confidence. It's a cycle: the more you know, the more you trust yourself to make decisions. And the more decisions you make, the more you learn from them.

This is the essence of the **knowledge-confidence loop**. The two feed into each other, building you up as you move forward. Sundar wasn't born knowing he would run Google. But with every success and every challenge, his confidence and knowledge both grew stronger. The real magic happens when you understand that these two—knowledge and confidence—aren't separate. They work hand in hand, pushing you to new heights.

Creating Your Own Knowledge-Confidence Loop

You can start building this loop for yourself, just like Sundar did. Begin with what you know. It doesn't have to be groundbreaking—just something you're good at. Maybe it's a specific skill at work, like problem-solving or managing projects. Or it could be a personal strength, like organizing events or staying calm under pressure. Use that knowledge as your foundation.

Next, take small actions to apply it. You don't need to wait for a big break to show what you can do. Just like Sundar trusted himself to push forward with Chrome, trust yourself to take that first step. The more you apply what you know, the more your confidence will grow. And as your confidence grows, so will your willingness to learn more. It's a cycle that keeps building on itself.

Here's a simple approach: for every new thing you learn, find a way to apply it within a week. Read a book? Try out one idea in your next meeting. Picked up a new skill? Use it in a small project. Don't wait until you feel like you know everything. Confidence comes from doing, not just learning.

Think about Sundar again. He didn't wait for someone else to validate his ideas. He took what he knew and ran with it, and in the process, learned even more. That's the loop in action—knowledge driving confidence, and confidence driving more knowledge.

Unleashing Potential Through Knowledge and Confidence

Success isn't just about what you know or how confident you feel—it's about combining the two in a way that fuels your actions. Whether you're in a meeting room, at a family gathering, or even facing personal challenges, knowing without confidence is like owning a treasure chest without the key. Likewise, having confidence without knowledge can make you feel ready to act, but without direction or clarity.

Let's think for a minute about what we've talked about. Merging knowledge with confidence isn't something that happens once; it's a continuous journey of learning, taking action, and reflecting on what we've done. Remember, Sundar Pichai didn't become a great leader in a day; your growth will take time too. With every step you take, no matter how big or small, you're building that important mix of knowledge and confidence.

The beauty of this formula is that it applies to every aspect of life. Whether you're looking to build a career, deepen relationships, or tackle personal goals, it's the synergy between what you know and how much you trust yourself that will keep pushing you forward.

At the heart of every achievement is the perfect blend of knowledge and confidence. This isn't a magic formula, but it is a reliable one. The more you learn, the more confident you become, and the more you believe in yourself, the more willing you are to learn and grow. It's a cycle that keeps feeding itself, building you up each time.

But remember: this process never really ends. There will always be new things to learn and new ways to stretch your confidence. The key is to embrace both learning and action as lifelong companions. Don't wait for the "perfect" moment to feel confident or know everything—start where you are, with what you have, and keep moving.

Let's put this into action. Think of one part of your life where you're holding back even though you know what to do, or where you feel confident but want to learn more. It could be something at work, a personal goal, or even a small change in how you deal with things.

For the next 30 days, focus on that area. Make a simple plan: what's one thing you can do this week to boost your confidence or learn more? Don't wait for the perfect time— just start.

At the end of the month, look back and see how far you've come. What's changed? How has balancing knowledge with confidence opened new doors for you? Remember, progress doesn't come from waiting—it comes from trusting yourself to take that next step.

Chapter 9

Bold Moves:
Thinking Big, Acting Bolder

It often starts at the dinner table. You're excitedly sharing an idea—maybe you want to start a food truck, become a musician, or change careers completely. Then, one of your relatives leans in, looks serious, and says, "Beta, be practical." Your dad might add, "There's no future in that. Why not think of something more stable, like becoming a doctor or an engineer?" You can see the excitement fade as they list all the risks and reasons why your idea won't work. Because in their eyes, real success is about stability, not chasing 'unrealistic' dreams.

Gradually, your big dream feels… impossible. You start thinking smaller and choose the safer path until one day, that dream is just a distant memory—filed under 'maybe someday.' But what if it's not your dream that's too big, but that 'practical advice' that's been holding you back all along?

The Art of Dreaming Big

It's a scene many of us know too well: an idea that feels huge and thrilling, but somehow, you find yourself shrinking it down, bit by bit, until it looks "practical." Maybe you once dreamed of opening a restaurant chain, but by the time everyone gave you their opinions, that dream became a small café, and then a part-time catering service. Or you pictured yourself on stage, but by the end of the conversation, it was reduced to singing at a local function once in a while. Before you know it, the dreams that made you excited are tucked away, shaped into something that feels safe enough for everyone else's comfort.

But big dreams aren't meant to be watered down. They're meant to make us feel a bit scared, encourage us to think outside the box, and inspire us to take bold leaps instead of just making small, cautious moves. When you set high goals, you challenge what's possible—not just for yourself, but for others who see you. Big dreams don't just change lives; they also shift perspectives and broaden what people believe can be achieved.

Think of Dr. Verghese Kurien, the man behind India's White Revolution. The idea of making India the top milk producer seemed impossible to many. People doubted him, saying, 'How can a country with milk shortages even dream of this?' But Kurien refused to scale down his vision. He believed in the power of cooperative dairy farming and took a leap that changed not only his life but also millions of others. He faced setbacks and disbelief, yet he kept his eyes on the bigger picture. Today, India is the top milk producer globally, all thanks to a man who refused to let a bold dream be minimized.

So, let go of the hesitation and think bigger. Picture the dream in its full glory—no edits, no modifications. Whether it's starting your own business or making a bold career change at 40, whatever your goal is, allow it room to grow. Dreaming big means stepping outside your comfort zone and exploring what's possible when you choose not to play it safe.

Big dreams push boundaries and stretch our limits. They force us to break free from the safe box we've built for ourselves. And when you hold onto them, without shrinking them to fit other people's expectations, you'll find that they act like a magnet—pulling you toward new opportunities, new people, and new ways of thinking.

Sure, people might call you impractical. They might suggest, "Why not aim a little lower?" or "Maybe stick to what you know." But that's the point—dreaming big is supposed to be uncomfortable. It's supposed to make you feel like you're biting off more than you can chew. That's where the magic lies: in stretching yourself so far that you discover just how much you're capable of.

So here's a thought: What if the only thing holding you back from achieving that 'impossible' dream isn't the lack of resources or the perfect timing, but the size of your vision? What if thinking big is the very first step toward making it real?

Because dreaming small won't make it happen. But daring to think boldly just might.

From Dreams to Plans

We all have big dreams—like starting a business, writing a book, or changing careers. However, these dreams can feel overwhelming when we don't know where to start. It's like standing at the bottom of a mountain, wondering, "How will I ever make it to the top?"

The truth is, big dreams aren't achieved all at once. They are built step by step, much like constructing a house. You wouldn't wake up to find a complete house built overnight. First, you dig the foundation, then lay each brick carefully. Eventually, you'll look up and see a home where there was once just an empty plot of land.

The same principle applies to any goal in life. Even the most successful individuals don't try to climb the entire mountain at once; they break it into smaller, manageable tasks. Take Ritesh Agarwal, the founder of OYO Rooms. He didn't begin with a huge hotel chain. He began with just one small guesthouse. He focused on understanding what travelers needed, then took small, thoughtful steps to expand from there. That's how he turned his dream into a reality—by focusing on the next immediate step, not the entire staircase.

So, how do you start chasing your big dreams? The first step is to get those thoughts out of your head and onto paper. Writing it down makes it feel real. Let's say you want to start a small business. Instead of stressing over everything you need to do, focus on what you can do right now. Maybe that means researching your market, setting up a little online store, or talking to someone who has been there for some advice. Here's how to start:

Set Clear Goals: What exactly do you want to achieve? Make it specific. Instead of saying, "I want to be successful," define what success looks like. Is it opening a small café? Launching a website? Getting fit? The clearer your goal, the easier it is to start.

Turn Goals into Small Tasks: If your goal is to open a café, don't start by trying to find the perfect location. Start smaller: find out what permits you need, talk to other café owners, or create a simple business plan. Each small step adds up.

Create a Timeline for Each Step: When do you want to achieve each step? Putting a rough timeframe keeps you focused without making it stressful.

Track Your Progress Regularly: Keep a simple checklist or a notebook. Every time you complete a small step, jot it down. You'd be surprised how motivating it is to see how far you've come. The key is not to let the big picture scare you. Focus on what's right in front of you—the next brick, the next step—and keep going.

Executing with Boldness

Once you have your plan ready, the real challenge starts: taking action. This is where many people freeze. You've put in the effort to prepare, but when it's time to go for it, fear kicks in. That nagging voice in your head says, "What if I mess up? What if everyone tells me I shouldn't have tried?" It can feel like a huge wall between where you are now and where you want to be.

But let's be honest—fear isn't something you can completely get rid of. It's a part of the process. What really matters is how you deal with it. Imagine Ritesh Agarwal again, after he had finally set up his first guest house. He could have stopped right there, satisfied with that small success. But his vision was bigger.

He kept pushing forward, using every small success to build momentum.

Every time he took a step, fear was right there, but he didn't let it hold him back. Being bold doesn't mean you're free from fear; it means you keep going even when you feel scared. Each time you act boldly, it's like building muscle— the more you do it, the stronger you get.

If you wait for fear to disappear, you might be waiting forever. It's normal to feel fear when trying something new, but it's important to keep moving forward. You need to practice taking action, even when you'd rather stay in your comfort zone.

Think for a moment: What bold move have you been putting off? Maybe it's sharing an idea at work, applying for a job you really want, or making a change in your life. Write it down and say it out loud. Then, break it into small steps. If you want to speak up more, try sharing one idea in your next meeting. If you're starting a side project, begin by doing some research. The first step doesn't have to be big; it just needs to move you forward.

Staying Steady Through Setbacks

Bold moves often come with their fair share of bumps along the way. We all know that sometimes things don't go as planned.

Maybe that big career change doesn't take off immediately, or your new business idea runs into some trouble. In those moments, it's easy to think, "Maybe this wasn't such a great idea." But hey, setbacks are totally normal; they don't mean you should throw in the towel. Just look at Ritesh Agarwal and his journey with OYO. He faced plenty of challenges—from hotels dropping out at the last minute to tough financial situations that made growth seem impossible. Each time, he had a choice: back down or keep pushing ahead. He chose to keep going. He learned from each bump in the road, adjusted his plans, and kept moving forward. That's what being bold is really about—it's not just about making daring choices; it's about staying committed when things don't go perfectly right away.

When you hit a wall, remember that it's not the end. It's just a chance to reevaluate and find another way. Instead of thinking, "This is a sign I should stop," ask yourself, "What's the next best move?" Sometimes that means changing your approach, and other times it means just pushing through until the breakthrough comes.

Action Steps for Boldness

Want to become bolder? Start small. Think of one area in your life where you've been holding back—maybe it's your job, your health, or a personal goal that feels a bit scary. Pick one easy step to take today, like making a phone call, signing up for a class, or asking someone for advice.

After you take that step, keep moving forward. At the end of each week, take a moment to reflect on what worked and what didn't. Write it down. This is how you grow—by thinking about your progress. The more you notice what helps you, the easier it will be to take your next step.

Then, choose a bigger goal—something that challenges you but still feels within reach. It could be sharing your ideas with your boss, starting a new project, or facing a challenge you've been avoiding. Make a rough plan, but stay flexible. Remember, being bold means taking steady steps, not rushing to finish.

The goal is to keep building on your bold actions, one step at a time, until what once seemed scary becomes natural. Every time you take action, no matter how small, you're training yourself to step out of your comfort zone. Soon, you'll be making moves you once thought were impossible.

Unleashing Potential Through Boldness

So, what's the takeaway? Success isn't limited to just dreaming big. Real progress happens when you turn those dreams into deliberate, bold actions. It means starting from where you are, using what you have, and challenging yourself to stretch your limits a bit further every time.

Think back to the start of this chapter—when we talked about that dinner table conversation where your dreams were reshaped to fit what's considered "safe" or "practical." Those voices—whether from others or your own doubts—will always be there. But here's the thing: choosing to step forward, to act courageously even when those voices linger, is entirely in your hands.

The path of thinking big and acting boldly isn't a one-time move. It's a constant loop: dream, act, reflect, and then dream even bigger. Each time you go through this cycle, you become stronger, more confident, and more aware of what you can truly achieve.

But this only works if you're willing to begin. So let's get started. Pick an area where you've been holding back—your career, health, or maybe a personal project that's been left on hold for too long. Create a plan: one bold step for today, a smaller move for this week, and a clear goal for the month ahead. Write it down, set reminders, and follow through.

Here's your challenge: stick with this plan for the next 30 days. Take steady actions toward that bold step, even if it feels a bit uneasy or uncertain. By the end of the month, look back and see what's changed—not just in your situation, but in how you view yourself.

The scale of your dreams determines the impact of your results. Don't let them shrink just because sticking to smaller ones feels easier. Dare to dream big, act boldly, and see where it takes you.

Chapter 10

Experience vs. Exposure – Expanding Horizons

We live in a world obsessed with #Experiences. The more exotic and impressive, the better. From weekend getaways to trying out the latest restaurant, it feels like everyone's competing to tick off more and more. Open Instagram or WhatsApp statuses, and it's full of people showing off a vacation here, a new hobby there, or the latest adventure sport. But what if these are just empty checkboxes? You could visit every restaurant in your city and still not call yourself a true foodie. You might hop from country to country without really seeing any of them. When the excitement fades, what do these experiences really mean?

Think back to the idea of chasing bold dreams that we explored in the last chapter—how the pressure to achieve something spectacular can shrink those dreams into safe, manageable goals. The same mindset creeps into how we think about experiences too. There's a constant push to do more, see more, be more, without pausing to ask if these experiences are adding true value.

It's tempting to think that the more we do, the more fulfilled we'll feel. But often, it's the opposite. Instead of getting something meaningful from these moments, we rush to the next thing, hoping to feel a sense of achievement. We attend conferences, read up on different topics, and try our hand at new projects—but it never really feels enough. Why? Because we confuse surface-level exposure with deep, real engagement.

Valuing Deep Engagement Over Simple Exposure

Let's look at the difference between exposure and true immersion. Imagine quickly flipping through headlines versus reading a single article thoroughly. The first is just a glance; the second is engagement. It's the same in life. We can fill our time with activities—watching TED talks, joining every new class, picking up new skills—thinking this will add up to something big. But in reality, it doesn't stick. Real growth happens when we focus deeply on a few things, take time to understand them, and then apply what we've learned.

Instead of doing everything, think of choosing just a few things and getting into them deeply. Remember, good judgment comes from experience, and experience comes from mistakes. We don't have to make every mistake ourselves; sometimes, exposure to others' experiences can save us from going down the wrong path. Like watching a close friend deal with a business failure—it's a reminder to be cautious when investing blindly. That's where exposure is useful: it's a heads-up to the potholes on the road ahead. But it's not the same as gaining firsthand knowledge through action.

Real growth doesn't happen from the sidelines. You can listen to countless stories of people climbing mountains, but until you've felt the strain in your own muscles or the chill of the wind at the peak, you won't know what it truly means to conquer one. That's the difference between knowing *of* something and *understanding* it.

Sometimes, we fill our days with too many activities—constantly jumping from one to the next, hoping to feel more accomplished. But true growth requires a shift in mindset. It's less about chasing after one new thing after another and more about staying with something long enough to understand its nuances. Like the artist who spends hours blending colors on a single canvas, or the writer who rewrites the same chapter until every word feels right. Mastery comes not from trying many things, but from a deep focus on a few.

Imagine an artist who decides to master watercolors instead of dabbling in every art form available. At first, they might be tempted to try sketching, sculpting, and digital art. But by choosing to stick with one, they learn to appreciate the subtleties of watercolor—the way the paint spreads on wet paper, the delicate control of brushstrokes, and the balance of water and pigment. Meanwhile, a jack-of-all-trades might have fun trying a bit of everything, but never truly understand any medium deeply.

This isn't just about art. Whether it's pursuing a career skill, developing a fitness routine, or building strong relationships—depth creates richness. Ask yourself: Are you adding years to your experience, or just adding more things to your schedule? It's easy to get busy, but it's depth that makes us grow.

One of the reasons people often mistake exposure for growth is because we believe more is always better. But think of it like tasting food—you don't have to eat an entire dish to know whether it's good or bad. Exposure is similar; it gives us a taste, a warning, or a recommendation. It tells us which paths might not be worth pursuing. Observing a friend's business failure teaches caution without having to lose money yourself. But to really learn the ropes of running a business, you need to be in it, handling your own ups and downs.

So, while exposure has its place, it's deep engagement that truly shapes us. One without the other is like having a map but never taking a step. The goal is to balance the two: learn from the paths others have taken, but walk your own to gain the wisdom that only comes from living it.

Pause for a moment and reflect: Are you spending your time getting to know things deeply, or are you rushing through life collecting snapshots? It's not about how much you do, but how deeply you engage. The answer might change how you approach your next big decision.

Pursuing Diverse Experiences

So, if true growth comes from deep engagement, does that mean sticking to just one path forever? Not at all. Deep engagement doesn't mean avoiding new things—it means embracing new experiences with the right mindset. The real magic happens when we step outside our comfort zones and explore unfamiliar places, roles, and perspectives, pushing ourselves beyond what we know.

That brings us to the next step: stepping outside of your comfort zone. Often, we stick to what feels familiar, thinking that a little bit of new exposure is enough to fuel growth. But true growth isn't about staying in safe territory and sampling new things—it happens when you push yourself into unknown, uncomfortable spaces. It's those challenging experiences, the ones that make your heart race and your mind scramble for footing, that leave a lasting impact.

Think about Bhuvan Bam. Today, he's known across India for his creative content, but it didn't start out smoothly. Back when YouTube was still new in India, Bhuvan had no idea how his videos would be received. His first few clips didn't get much attention, and every time he uploaded, there was the fear of what people would say. But he didn't let that uncertainty hold him back. He embraced those uncomfortable early days, experimenting with different formats, learning from both praise and criticism, and steadily improving his craft. By repeatedly stepping outside his comfort zone, he found his unique voice and style.

The discomfort he experienced wasn't a sign to stop. It was a sign of growth. Real growth doesn't happen when everything feels easy and smooth—it's when things get tough, when you're uncertain, and yet, you decide to keep moving forward. Each time Bhuvan pushed himself, he learned something new—not just about content creation, but about what resonates with his audience, what makes people laugh, and what doesn't. That exposure to unfamiliar territories helped him shape the creator he is today.

But not every new experience has to be a leap into the unknown like Bhuvan's. Sometimes, we gain exposure through smaller steps—by observing others, reading up, or simply staying curious. We may not always get a chance to dive into everything firsthand, but learning from the experiences of others helps bridge that gap.

When I first started working with global teams, I didn't have direct experience with European or Latin American cultures. I wasn't familiar with their work styles, decision-making approaches, or even basic office etiquette. At the time, jumping into those environments directly would have felt overwhelming. Instead, I spent time getting exposure—talking to colleagues from different regions, observing how they approached problems, and reading up on cultural differences. This exposure didn't make me an expert overnight, but it prepared me to handle the nuances when I finally had to lead diverse teams.

It's the same reason we turn to specialists—doctors, lawyers, or consultants—when we're unsure of something. They provide the exposure we lack and guide us when we're navigating unfamiliar ground. Even when we seek second or third opinions in complex medical cases, we're expanding our understanding through the perspectives of others. This way, exposure offers a glimpse of the road ahead, helping us make better decisions when we have to chart the path ourselves.

The goal is to gain as much direct experience as we can while also building exposure to areas where firsthand knowledge isn't possible. Learning from colleagues, mentors, or even books expands our awareness, making it easier to adapt when the time comes to take the lead ourselves.

Living Fully

If true growth comes from deeply connecting with things, how do we ensure we're building a life that feels meaningful? It's not simply doing more. It's picking the right experiences— ones that leave us with a sense of purpose, not just busyness. Real fulfillment doesn't come from ticking off checklists; it's in the small, everyday choices we make. Think about your daily routine. Does it bring value, or does it feel like a series of tasks to complete? We often assume that being busy means we're accomplishing something, but real satisfaction comes from making time for what really matters.

This doesn't mean giving up routines. They give us stability. But it's finding a balance between the everyday stuff and those activities that bring joy, challenge us, or teach us something new. Even simple things—trying out a new recipe in the kitchen, reading a thought-provoking book, or spending a relaxed evening chatting with family—can add depth to our lives. These are moments that social media posts can never capture. Living fully is less about the number of things we do and more about the quality of those experiences.

Think of a parent wanting to guide their child. They might not have experienced everything firsthand, but if they've been exposed to different situations, they'll have a better understanding. Without a blend of personal experiences and exposure to others' stories, how can they help their child navigate life's ups and downs? It's like wanting to show someone a path through a forest without ever having walked it yourself or even seen a map of the terrain.

It's not just for parents. Whether we're trying to guide our kids, mentoring someone younger, or simply making decisions for ourselves, this mix of what we know and what we've learned from others becomes crucial. It's easy to think living fully means grand achievements like starting a business or going on a long trip abroad. But some of the richest experiences happen in small, quiet moments. It could be as simple as learning a new dish, taking up gardening, or reconnecting with old friends. These may not seem flashy, but they bring a satisfaction that's hard to find in big, dramatic gestures.

Think of the saying, "Life isn't measured by the number of breaths we take, but by the moments that take our breath away." Living fully means creating these special moments for ourselves—ones that might not stand out to others but hold deep meaning for us. So, how do we begin to live in a way that feels richer and more fulfilling? One approach is to make a "Life Experience List." Not the typical 'bucket list' of far-off goals, but a collection of things—big or small—that you want to try. Think of it as a guide for choosing what adds joy and meaning to your days.

Start small—write down things you've always wanted to do. Maybe it's learning to cook a new dish, visiting a new place, picking up a skill you've been thinking about. It doesn't have to be something huge. Even small joys, like watching the sunrise in a new spot or trying your hand at a hobby you've been curious about, can make a big difference.

Our routines are necessary, but they shouldn't fill up our days completely. If your schedule is packed with things that feel like they're just draining your energy, swap one of those out for something that makes you feel more alive. Trade an evening of mindless TV scrolling for a long-overdue call to a friend. Or replace a repetitive weekend chore with an hour learning a new craft or revisiting an old passion.

Living fully isn't about crowding every hour with activities—it's about picking the right ones. It's making sure that each day, whether packed with work, rest, or something exciting, leaves us feeling a little more connected to who we are and what we value. That's what turns a busy routine into a life that feels truly meaningful.

Chapter 11

Steady Mind, Steady Life

We're always told to keep doing more and aiming higher. On the outside, everything might look fine—good job, bills paid, family doing okay, and things going smoothly. But deep inside, many of us feel restless. It's like there's a buzzing feeling that never goes away, like a phone stuck on vibrate. We keep running around, always busy, yet never really feeling calm.

We all know someone like this. Maybe it's you. Maybe it's a co-worker who's always cheerful and on top of everything. Or maybe it's a friend who posts smiling pictures of family dinners and trips, never showing any problems. But if you sit with them for a cup of chai and really ask how they're doing, the truth might be very different—full of stress, worry, and a mind that won't slow down.

Balancing work, family, and social expectations can be tough. On the outside, we might look fine, but inside, it can feel like we're drowning. Whether it's meeting deadlines, caring for parents, or making life decisions, staying calm often gets pushed aside. But as we've seen, it's not about doing more or achieving bigger goals. What really matters is the quality of our experiences and staying steady inside as we go through them.

The real challenge isn't the daily tasks—it's the restless mind. When our mind is all over the place, even small issues can feel huge.

A calm mind is like a still lake. Regardless of the chaos around us, a clear surface reflects everything accurately. However, when our minds are restless, it's like a lake with choppy waters—distorted and unable to show things as they truly are. This is why two people can face the same challenge—one may crumble, while the other remains strong. The difference isn't in the problem but in the stability of the mind facing it.

So, while we can't control everything happening outside, what we can control is how steady we stay on the inside. Building this inner calm happens by finding a way to be truly strong—not by changing everything around us, but by becoming unshakeable no matter what happens. And for that, we need to start working on the one thing we usually ignore: our own minds.

The Concept of Inner Calm

But why does inner calm matter so much? It's because a steady mind is like an anchor. It keeps us steady, regardless of how intense the storm gets. When we're calm, we can see things clearly—without the distortion of panic, stress, or fear. This clarity helps us think clearly, make quick decisions, and stay focused, even when life gets chaotic. This kind of stability doesn't come from trying to control everything around us; it comes from learning to stay centered, no matter the circumstances.

A calm mind isn't a luxury; it's a necessity. When everything around us feels chaotic, with thoughts racing and stress overwhelming us, staying steady becomes our greatest strength. A steady mind goes beyond feeling good; it enables us to think clearly, act wisely, and make the best decisions, even when things seem to be falling apart. With a calm mind, we can see situations as they truly are, rather than how they appear in the heat of the moment.

Take those days when nothing goes as planned. The meetings run late, a project hits a dead end, your child throws a tantrum at the worst possible time and you're bombarded with calls from home—all at once. It's tempting to react, to let the frustration show. The minute you lose your cool, minor hiccups turn into a full-blown crisis, and decisions made in a rush almost always end up causing more trouble. On the other hand, if you manage to keep your mind steady, you learn to pause in the middle of traffic chaos to notice the openings between cars. That calm allows you to move forward without getting stuck in the gridlock.

This clarity isn't just about dealing with office stress or daily annoyances; it applies to all areas of life, from managing relationships to handling bigger challenges. When we stay centered, we don't let emotions like anger, fear, or anxiety dictate our responses. We choose to respond rather than react. Think about a time when you remained calm while others were losing their cool, or when you guided a loved

 COACHING FOR A LIFE WELL-LIVED

one through an argument without getting swept up in the moment's heat. How did that affect the outcome? How did it make you feel afterward? This inner calm doesn't mean you're ignoring the problem; it means you're facing it without letting it overwhelm you.

This isn't just theory. History shows us examples of people who stayed calm in the face of major challenges. Think of those who seem unshakeable—no matter what happens, they maintain their composure. Mahatma Gandhi is a great example; he remained steady during some of history's toughest times. When things got hard and people opposed him, he didn't react without thinking. He stayed calm and chose his actions with patience. It's not that he didn't feel angry or upset—he just didn't let those feelings control what he did.

This ability to stay steady doesn't mean shutting out emotions. It's about choosing how you react. And that's what makes a calm mind so powerful—it helps you see beyond the immediate chaos and respond in ways that don't make tough situations worse. Because the truth is, we can't control every problem that comes our way. But with a steady mind, we don't have to.

Foundations of Mental Stability

If staying calm is like having an anchor, how do we build it? It starts with habits that help us stay steady, no matter what's happening around us. One good way to begin is by practicing mindfulness. This doesn't mean sitting cross-legged for hours. It's about staying present, whether you're sipping your morning chai or handling a busy day. When your mind drifts, this practice brings your focus back to what's happening right now, instead of worrying about tomorrow or thinking of the past.

Start small. Spend a few minutes each morning sitting comfortably and focus on your breathing. Notice the air going in and out. Your mind will wander, and that's normal. Gently bring it back each time. Even a few minutes like this can help you feel calmer and more focused as you begin your day.

Another easy way to practice mindfulness is to watch your thoughts without reacting to them. Imagine standing by a busy road. You don't have to follow each car or get lost in the noise. Just notice the cars passing by. It's the same with thoughts—let them come and go without running after them. This' helps you step back, so you're not reacting right away and can see things more clearly.

Let me tell you the story of the elephant and a fly. Imagine a majestic elephant standing beneath a sprawling tree, leisurely nibbling on leaves. Suddenly, a tiny fly zooms near its ear, buzzing loudly. The elephant, with a gentle flick of its ears, tries to shoo it away. But the pesky fly returns, determined to disrupt the elephant's peace.Frustrated, the elephant finally turns to the fly and asks, "Why can't you just relax? Why are you so restless?"

The fly replies, "I am pulled by everything around me. I go wherever I hear, see, or smell something interesting. My senses control my attention, and I cannot help but flit around."

The elephant, on the other hand, stays calm and focused. "I am in charge of where my attention goes. My senses do not rule me. When I eat, I am completely immersed in eating. That's why I am peaceful. I control my attention, and this helps me stay calm and steady."

In life, we have a choice: to let every distraction pull us like the fly, or to be like the elephant—calm and steady, choosing where our mind goes instead of reacting to everything around us. If we allow every little noise or event to control our thoughts, we'll always feel restless and scattered. But if we direct our attention and choose where to focus, we can bring our minds to a state of peace, no matter what's buzzing around us.

Establishing simple daily routines can further build this mental steadiness. Something as small as a morning walk, a few minutes of journaling, or setting a daily intention can serve as anchors for our mind. These little habits create pockets of calm, even when life feels hectic. They help build a mind that doesn't waver at every buzz, but remains centered, no matter what.

Beyond routines, mental clarity comes from simplifying our thoughts. When our minds are full of worries, old grudges, and endless to-do lists, even small problems can feel too much to handle. To fix this, start letting go of thoughts that don't help—like replaying mistakes or stressing over things you can't control. Forgiving and letting go isn't only a kind thing to do; it also clears up space in your mind. Holding onto grudges or regrets is like filling a room with junk—there's no room to move. But when we let go, our minds become calmer and clearer.

Each day, take a moment to think about what went well. Remember the good conversations, the little wins, or even times when you stayed patient. Gratitude isn't just a word—it helps train your mind to see what's good, instead of focusing only on what's wrong. Doing this regularly makes your mind stronger, like adding layers to your calm, so bigger problems won't shake you as easily.

When we clear our thoughts and focus on the present, we start seeing changes—not only in how we feel but in how we react to the world. Like an elephant choosing where to focus, we can guide our minds away from distractions and towards what truly matters. Bit by bit, this stability becomes our greatest strength when life's challenges come up.

Harnessing Emotional Intelligence

A steady mind isn't only staying calm on the outside; it's also recognizing and managing what's going on inside. This involves our emotions. Sometimes we act quickly because we're angry or hold back because we're scared, and our feelings can take over before we realize it. It's normal to react like this, but we can learn to control how we respond instead.

Think of the times when frustration or anxiety clouded your judgment. Sometimes we argue with coworkers and say things we regret. Other times, we let self-doubt stop us from taking chances that could open new doors. Emotions can shape our choices without us even noticing, and we end up making decisions that don't really match what we want.

The key is to practice emotional intelligence. It doesn't mean ignoring emotions, but understanding them. When we pause and notice what we're feeling—whether it's anger, fear, or excitement—we give ourselves a moment to decide, "Do I want to react now, or is there a better way?"

This is what emotional intelligence is all about: seeing our emotions for what they are, but not letting them control what we do.

Start small. The next time you feel frustrated or anxious, pause for a second before you respond. Ask yourself, "What am I feeling right now?" Naming the emotion—whether it's stress, fear, or excitement—creates a little space between what you feel and what you do. And in that space, you get to choose whether to react right away or pause and respond calmly.

Over time, this practice changes how you handle tense situations. Instead of snapping back in an argument or missing out on something good out of fear, you'll find yourself pausing, assessing, and responding in a way that feels true to you. It's not about ignoring your emotions—it's training yourself to step back and decide how to act.

To achieve this, it helps to identify what triggers you. It might be a specific tone that annoys you or the fear of failing that holds you back from trying new things. Understanding your emotional triggers makes it easier to handle those situations.

One way to do this is by practicing "thought distancing." Picture yourself standing by a busy road, watching cars speed by. Each car is a thought—some zooming, some blaring their horns, some just passing. Instead of stepping into traffic, stay on the side and watch. There's no need to follow each car or get caught up in the noise. It's the same with emotions. When you feel anger or anxiety bubbling up, picture it as one of those cars. Instead of jumping into the chaos, step back mentally and watch it pass. You're not ignoring the feeling— you're just giving yourself a moment to decide if it's worth following.

Let's say your boss criticizes your work suddenly. The instant reaction might be defensiveness or self-doubt. But instead of responding right away, try stepping back and naming it: "I feel upset right now." Just recognizing it can loosen its grip on you. Then, instead of reacting defensively, you can ask yourself, "What's the most useful way to handle this?" That brief pause is where real emotional control starts.

One way to build this habit is by keeping an emotional journal. For a week, jot down moments when your emotions run high. Note what triggered it, how you reacted, and what you could have done differently. Don't worry about perfect words—it's just for you. When you look back, you'll notice patterns: maybe anger spikes when you're tired, or anxiety flares up before big meetings. Spotting these patterns helps you be more prepared.

Ask yourself: How would things have been different if you'd been calmer? Would the outcome have changed? Over time, this practice helps you recognize that space between feeling and reacting more often. That's where true emotional strength builds.

Achieving a steady mind is a journey. It's like building a muscle—slow, steady, and requiring patience. But each small step—whether it's pausing before reacting, practicing mindfulness, or letting go of old worries—brings you closer to a mind that can face any challenge without wavering.

Impulsivity might be human, but choosing how to respond is a skill.Remember the story of the elephant and the fly. Inner peace isn't about blocking out the noise around us—it's deciding where to direct our focus. When you control your attention, you're in charge of your reactions. True inner calm is built not in a single moment but through small, consistent habits that keep us grounded every day. When you choose where your focus goes, you choose your peace.

Chapter 12

Choices and Destiny –
Your Story, Your Way

We make choices every day. Some are small. Some have the power to change everything. Choosing a career, deciding to move to a new city, or even handling things when they don't go as planned. It feels like we're in control, doesn't it? But is it really that simple?

Think back to those times when, no matter how hard you tried, things didn't turn out the way you hoped. Maybe you spent months preparing for an entrance exam like JEE, only to face disappointment. Or perhaps you went into a campus interview confident you'd get the job but walked out with a rejection instead. It could be that you were sure you'd earn that promotion, but it slipped through your fingers. Or a relationship you believed would last forever fell apart unexpectedly.

And then, there are the surprises—the job offer you never saw coming, a career change you hadn't planned, or meeting someone who suddenly opens up a world of opportunities.

There are months when life feels stuck, when nothing seems to happen. And then, in just a week, everything shifts.

It makes you wonder—how much of our story is really in our hands, and how much is influenced by things we can't see? From the moment we start making decisions, we carry invisible weights—our upbringing, what society expects of us, our own fears and doubts. These shape how we move through life, often without us even realizing. Sometimes, the path we think we're choosing isn't entirely our own.

Life is unpredictable. Even when everything is carefully planned, one sudden change can turn it all upside down. But here's the paradox—those moments of failure or disappointment often open doors we didn't even know existed. They push us in directions we might have never chosen but somehow make sense later. While we can't always control what happens, we do have a choice in how we respond to it. That's where our power lies.

Every chapter in this book has explored this bigger question in its own way. We've talked about building confidence, finding courage, bouncing back from setbacks, and staying resilient when it's easier to quit. But underneath it all, there's been this constant tug-of-war between what's in our hands and what's already decided. Where does the line blur? How much control do we really have over the direction of our lives?

The answer doesn't lie in theories or philosophies. It's found in the choices made when life knocks us down, in those moments when we keep moving forward even when every sign seems to say, "Stop." It's in these times that we realize—our story isn't defined by a single decision. It's defined by how we handle what life throws our way.

Destiny and Choice

But where does our effort end, and destiny take over? It's a question that has shaped countless stories, myths, and everyday lives. It's a question that makes us pause and reflect on our own paths. Is everything that happens in our control, or are we sometimes carried along by forces beyond our reach?

Life is like a flowing river. The current represents everything we can't control—circumstances, people's opinions, luck. . But the strokes we take as we move through it are like the choices we make. We may not decide the direction of the current, but we decide when to push forward, when to adjust, and when to let go. Sometimes, no matter how strong your strokes are, the river finds its own path. Yet, it's how you keep moving, even when the current feels too strong, that defines your journey. It's this balance—between choice and destiny—that shapes who we are.

Take someone like Steve Jobs. Despite being removed from the company he co-founded, he came back stronger, leading it to even greater success. His setback wasn't the end; it was the start of a bigger opportunity. Or think about Mary Kom, the Indian boxer. Despite facing societal expectations and financial hardships, she pursued her passion and broke barriers in a male-dominated sport. Her journey, like ours, wasn't a straight path. Yet, each decision shaped her legacy.

Throughout history, whether in modern times or centuries ago, people have faced similar crossroads where their choices and circumstances intertwined. Just like Steve Jobs and Mary Kom navigated unexpected turns to create their legacies, ancient stories from the Mahabharata and beyond also reveal how individuals balanced destiny and decision-making.

This idea of balance—between choice and destiny—is woven into many stories and lives. Take the *Mahabharata*, for example. Karna's loyalty and strength were overshadowed by his birth, while Eklavya's talent was marked by his act of sacrifice. And then there's Siddhartha Gautama. Born as a prince and expected to become king, his destiny shifted when he chose a path of spiritual enlightenment, becoming Gautama Buddha.Each of them made choices that reflected their values, but they didn't control where those choices led. Their efforts shaped their legacies, but destiny played its own part in deciding how they would be remembered.

But does that mean their efforts were in vain? Not at all. Karna's story became one of resilience, and Eklavya is remembered for his strength of character. Their choices still mattered, even when the path wasn't theirs to control.

It's the same for us. When things don't go as planned, it doesn't mean we lose the power to choose how we react. Maybe your career takes a turn you didn't expect. Maybe a goal feels out of reach. Or maybe life just goes in a completely different direction. It's easy to feel like everything's slipping away. But that's when the choices we make matter the most. It's less about where you end up and more about whether you decide to keep going.

Think of a parent who's juggling work and family responsibilities. They might feel overwhelmed, pulled in every direction. Or consider someone feeling stuck in a job that doesn't bring joy anymore. These are familiar struggles. Yet, it's often in these moments of uncertainty that we find the courage to make choices that lead to growth, even if the path forward isn't clear right away.

It's these everyday decisions that remind us that even when life feels uncertain, each choice we make has the power to shift our direction.

Take a moment to reflect on three times in your life when things didn't turn out as planned. Write them down. What choices did you make afterward? How did those choices shape where you are today? Did they lead you down an unexpected but fulfilling path, or did they teach you something you needed to know?

Tackling Uncertainties with Destiny in Mind

Life is full of surprises. No matter how much we plan, things rarely go exactly as expected. Yet, we keep pushing forward, hoping our efforts will take us where we want to go. But success and failure are like two sides of the same coin—there's no one without the other. And just when you think you have it figured out, life spins the coin again.

We've all seen people achieve big goals with what seems like little effort, while others struggle and give their all, only to fall short. It's frustrating to pour yourself into something and watch others succeed in half the time. In moments like these, it's easy to feel defeated and ask yourself, "*Why not me?*". It's a feeling that most of us have faced, especially when we've done everything right and still come up short.

But that's where destiny steps in. You can give your best, but sometimes the results just don't match the effort. Does that mean your hard work didn't matter? Not at all. Maybe it's leading you somewhere better, somewhere you haven't even thought of yet. The problem is, we get so stuck on what went wrong that we fail to notice what's coming next. Dwelling on a few setbacks can blind you to new chances knocking at your door. So, no matter how many times you stumble, you have to keep moving forward—with courage, passion, and perseverance.

Let's take a moment to think about how we react when things don't go as planned. Imagine Anil, a young professional who decided to leave his engineering job to chase his passion for teaching. At first, things didn't work out the way he hoped. He struggled with financial instability and felt the weight of societal judgment. But instead of giving up, he took small steps—earning certifications, volunteering to gain experience, and building a network of like-minded people. It wasn't easy, and there were many moments of doubt. But each step brought him closer to the life he truly wanted. Anil's journey wasn't about having everything figured out. It was about trusting the process and taking each step with intention.

Think back to moments in your life when things didn't go as planned. Maybe it was a job you didn't get, a relationship that didn't work out, or a personal goal that felt out of reach. What choices did you make afterward? Did they lead you down a different, perhaps even more fulfilling path? Or did they teach you something valuable about yourself and what you truly want?

Sometimes, a setback can be the very thing that pushes us to grow.

I remember a story I once heard: A father talking to his son, who was on the verge of quitting. *'Dad, I'm not getting anywhere. Maybe it's just not meant to be.'* The father replied, *'Everyone has a dream. But if you give up when it's tough, those dreams turn into regrets. Quitting might feel easier now, but it turns your days into a routine without purpose.'*

His words struck a chord, and they should for all of us too. Giving up may end the struggle today, but it also ends the possibility of success tomorrow. When life takes a turn we didn't expect, holding onto disappointment won't change what happened. But using it to build strength will. If setbacks feel like dead ends, take a step back and focus on what's still in your hands—your response, your willingness to keep going.

The next time life takes a turn you didn't expect, instead of holding onto disappointment, try seeing what you can learn. It's not always easy, but shifting your perspective can make a big difference. Think of a recent challenge—how did you respond? Did you give in to frustration, or did you look for a way forward? Reflecting on these moments helps us grow and prepares us for future challenges.

Success and failure don't look the same for everyone. For one student, passing an exam might be a huge win. For another, getting 95% might feel like a failure because they were aiming for 99%. It's not really about the results. What matters is what you learn and how you grow along the way. So instead of thinking, "Why is this happening to me?" try looking at it differently. There's usually a bigger picture that's hard to see right now. Ask yourself, "What's one small thing I can change today?" or "What's one step I can take to turn things around?" Because if you're busy looking back, you'll miss what's right in front of you.

Success isn't defined by a single standard. It's about what matters to you personally. What truly counts is having the courage to keep moving forward, even if your journey looks different from someone else's.

The challenges we go through shape us. But what really makes a difference is how we use those experiences to build something that lasts.

That's where the idea of a legacy comes in—not just living, but living in a way that stands for something meaningful.

Crafting a Legacy within Destiny's Framework

We all want to leave something behind, to be remembered in a way that lasts beyond our time. But a legacy isn't built overnight—it's made up of countless, intentional decisions that come together over time. Every small action we take creates ripples that move through our lives, touching others and shaping the world around us. So, instead of chasing what others say is success, think about the kind of life you want to create. What values do you want to be remembered for? What story do you want your life to tell?

Think of the relationships you build, the things you learn, the experiences you cherish, and the emotions that shape you. These four pillars—relationships, learning, experiences, and emotions—are what give life its depth. They make everything more meaningful and create a sense of wholeness. When you choose actions that strengthen these areas, you're not just living for today—you're building something that lasts. Strengthening these pillars is at the heart of coaching for life.

Small actions have a lot of power. Supporting a friend when it's hard, choosing honesty when it's easier to hide, or showing kindness when you could look the other way—these choices might feel small at the moment, but they are the very things that shape the legacy you're building. People don't remember the titles you held or the awards you won; they remember how you made them feel, the values you stood by, and the strength you showed when times were tough.

Success and failure play a role, but the essence lies in crafting a life filled with meaning and purpose. It's about building something that transcends titles and awards. Like a stone dropped into a still pond, each decision you make sends ripples that can touch lives you may never encounter. This is why it's vital to reflect on what you want your life to represent. Whether serving as a support for your family, mentoring those just starting out, or living with integrity, your legacy begins with the small, everyday choices you make.

So, take a moment to reflect on your own story. What small, deliberate choices can you make today that bring you closer to the life you want to build? It could be reaching out to someone you admire, learning a new skill, or spending time with loved ones. Each step, no matter how small, shapes the person you become.

If you're unsure where to start, think of the different areas that make up your life—like your career, relationships, health, and personal growth. Focus on one of these areas each month. It doesn't have to be a major change; even small shifts, like dedicating time to something meaningful, can make a difference. Whether it's strengthening a bond with a loved one, exploring something you're curious about, or taking small steps toward a goal, these moments add up. Over time, these actions create a pattern—a habit of growth and intention.

As you reflect on these areas, you'll start to see how these simple, thoughtful choices connect, building momentum and showing you the path forward.

If you want to start somewhere, try keeping a "Legacy Journal." It doesn't have to be fancy—just a notebook where you write down your thoughts, what's important to you, and what kind of impact you want to have. Think about the values you want to live by. And each month, make one small choice that lines up with that. It could be helping someone, sharing something you've learned, or just staying true to your word. All those small choices really add up over time.

A year from now, take a look back and see how far you've come.

Because at the end of the day, success isn't reaching a finish line or hitting a milestone. It's living in a way that feels true to you, knowing you've made a difference. It's being able to look back and feel proud of the life you've built, even in the face of challenges.

If there's one thing to take away from this book, it's that life isn't just about the goals we hit or the milestones we reach. It's really about how we live each day and the values we hold onto, no matter what. Coaching, like I've talked about in these chapters, isn't just about helping someone "succeed." It's about showing them what they're capable of, helping them make choices they're proud of, and building a life that means something.

Your story isn't just about where you end up. It's shaped by every choice you make and every time you decide to keep going, no matter what. So whether life's going smoothly or feels uncertain, whether you're celebrating or struggling, remember: You have the power to decide where things go from here.

As you finish reading this, challenge yourself. Try making one small decision each month that brings you closer to the life you want. It could be anything—reaching out to someone, learning something new, or pushing yourself a little bit more. Let each step remind you that this journey is *yours* to create.

Destiny might have its own plans, but it's your choices that really shape your life. We can't always control what happens, but we can decide how we handle it. That's what living a meaningful life is all about—owning each step, staying true to who you are, and creating something that really matters.

So if you remember one thing, let it be this: *Your story is yours to write.* Every step, every choice, is a chance to live fully and build something real. Take what you've learned, and go live a life that truly feels like *yours*.

Author Bio

Sudhir Dasamantharao is a dedicated coach and author with years of global experience guiding individuals through personal and professional transformations. With a background in finance and leadership roles across diverse industries like IT, banking, manufacturing, and consulting, Sudhir has honed his skills in understanding the nuances of human potential. His passion for coaching stems from a deep commitment to helping others find balance, purpose, and fulfillment in their lives.

Coaching for A Life Well-Lived is his debut book, offering practical strategies, real-life stories, and actionable tools designed to support readers through different phases of life. Sudhir is dedicated to empowering individuals to create lives that reflect their core values, helping them discover purpose and meaning while living authentically.